EMMELINE PANKHURST

Emmeline Pankhurst was the most prominent campaigner for women's right to vote and was transformed into a popular heroine of the early twentieth century. Early in life she was attracted to socialism, then she grew into an entrenched and militant suffragette and ended up as a Conservative Party candidate. This new biography examines the guiding principles that underpinned all of Emmeline Pankhurst's actions, and places her achievements within a wider social and political context.

In this well-structured, fluent and lively account, Paula Bartley uses new archival material to assess whether Pankhurst should be seen as a heroine or a tyrant, a conservative or a progressive.

Paula Bartley is Senior Lecturer in History at the University of Wolverhampton. She has published widely on women in history, notably *Votes for Women* (Hodder, 1998) and *Prostitution: Prevention and Reform in England* (Routledge, 2000).

ROUTLEDGE HISTORICAL BIOGRAPHIES

SERIES EDITOR: ROBERT PEARCE

Routledge Historical Biographies provide engaging, readable and academically credible biographies written from an explicitly historical perspective. These concise and accessible accounts will bring important historical figures to life for students and general readers alike.

In the same series:

EMMELINE PANKHURST

Paula Bartley

LONDON AND NEW YORK

First published 2002
by Routledge
11 New Fetter Lane, London EC4P 4EE

Simultaneously published in the USA and Canada
by Routledge
29 West 35th Street, New York, NY 10001

Routledge is an imprint of the Taylor & Francis Group

Typeset in Garamond and Scala by Taylor & Francis Books Ltd
Printed and bound in Great Britain by Biddles Ltd, Guildford and
King's Lynn

British Library Cataloguing in Publication Data
A catalogue record for this book is available from the British Library

Library of Congress Cataloging in Publication Data
A catalog record for this book has been requested

ISBN 0–415–20650–2 (hbk)
ISBN 0–415–20651–0 (pbk)

For Reka Dudley and Olivia Hockridge

CONTENTS

PLATES

ACKNOWLEDGEMENTS

I owe a huge debt to a number of people. Robert Pearce's critical acumen combined with his generosity of spirit made him the ideal editor. I should also like to thank Vicky Peters at Routledge for her careful reading of the text and her reassurance. I was fortunate to meet Michael Foot, whose late wife Jill Craigie had researched extensively into the lives of the suffragettes. Michael Foot was extraordinarily generous with his time, and I thank him for all the insights he shared with me. In the midst of her own research Karen Hunt generously read and commented most helpfully on my chapter on the ILP and socialist women. Diane Atkinson, Elizabeth Crawford and Angela V. John provided advice on sources and Myrna Goode and the late Philip Goode gave me access to their collection. Bill Bartley gave his time generously to help with research in the west of England. Colleagues and friends at the University of Wolverhampton were characteristically helpful and encouraging: Marie-Clare Balaam, Eva Kolinsky, Janis Lomas, Peter Neville, Phil Knowles, Rosie Miles, Lesley Tennick, Fiona Terry-Chandler and Malcolm Wanklyn among them. Special thanks to Pat Green, Martin Durham and Ginny Hartley, who all made very useful comments on various chapters, and to John Benson and Laura Ugolini, who read the complete manuscript and made many numerous suggestions for improvement. The Women's History Unit at the University of Wolverhampton gave me encouragement when I most needed it. My heartfelt thanks to all of you.

Many librarians and archivists offered invaluable help and I would like to thank them all. David Doughan, Fawcett Library; the British Library; Cambridge University Library; Colindale Newspaper Library; House of Lords Library; London School of Economics archive; the Public Record Office at Kew, especially Sheila Gopaulen; the Bodleian and especially Vivien Bradley; the National Register of Archives; Pankhurst Centre, Manchester, especially Emilli Doran; Greater Manchester Record Office; Manchester Register Office, particularly Jeffrey Adams; the staff of the Local Studies Unit and Social Science Library of the Manchester Central Library; Salford Local History, Salford; Pump House Archive and Museum, Manchester; John Rylands Library, Deansgate; John Rylands University Campus Library, Manchester; Salford Record Office; Salford University Library; Rochdale Local Studies Library; Working Class Movement Library, Salford, particularly Alain Kahan; the Portico Library, Manchester, particularly Ed Potten; and the Manchester Literary and Philosophical Society, particularly Stella Lowe; Gail Cameron at the Museum of London; Verity Andrews at the University of Reading Archives; and the library staff at the University of Wolverhampton.

My research involved using archives outside of England. When I visited the Isle of Man to research Emmeline Pankhurst's early life, many people shared their extensive knowledge with me. I am hugely indebted to Helen Leigh, who taught me Manx history, offered generous hospitality and put me in touch with Miss M. Critchlow, Roger Sims, Priscilla Lewthwaite and Mr Cowen, all of whom helped me with Emmeline Pankhurst's genealogical history. In particular, I would like to thank the Manx historian Patricia de Ban for her help on Emmeline's early life and her comments on my first chapter. My Canadian research was helped by a travel grant from the British Association for Canadian Studies and I would like to thank them for making my trip possible. I am grateful to a number of Canadians, especially Arthur and Doreen Gryfe, Larry McNally, Ghislain Malette, Judith Emery, Yuri Shimpo and Tom Tytor. Thanks also to Angus McLaren for his advice via the internet, which helped me trace the Canadian Social Hygiene Council; to Dawn Lemain for giving me permission to quote from her father Bill McNeill's recordings and to Margorie McEnaney for her interview with Nellie Hall Humpherson. While in Canada I made a number of friends, including Jeanette Neeson, Doug Hay, Mary Jane Mossman, Brian Bucknall and Peter and Flora Kelly, all of whom provided emotional sustenance as well as intellectual inspiration. Thanks to Sian Miles for introducing me to some of them. I was awarded a month's British Studies Fellowship by the Harry Ransom Center at the University of Texas. I should like to thank them and Roger Louis, Patricia Kruppa and the audience of the British Studies Seminar for their help and advice. During my visit, Lesley Hall, a true internationalist, put me in contact with Hal Smith and Judy McArthur, who generously shared their expertise on the American suffrage movement with me and provided the most delightful evening in Austin, Texas.

I owe a huge debt to Rachel Eckersley for helping with me with the research on Emmeline Pankhurst's early political life. In turn, many individuals gave her invaluable help and I would like to thank Douglas Farnie, John Smethurst, David Jeremy, Rev. Dr Len Smith, Neil and Sue Richardson, Mike Rose, Rev. Keith Archer, Anne Cansell, Roy Cuthbert, Lucy and Mike Howells, Helen Pussard and Ross Eckersley for their advice.

Family and family friends helped in all sorts of ways. I would especially like to thank Trevor Bowen and Sara Lean, Rob and Liz Dudley, Chris and Viv Kelly and Cathy Loxton for putting me up and putting up with me when

I was researching in London. Hilary Bourdillon, Urszula Clark, David and Jane Carpanini and Ann Swarbrick deserve thanks for their continuing interest in the book. My greatest thanks, as ever, go to my husband, Jonathan Dudley, who helped me with my research in America and Canada, read and commented on numerous drafts and more importantly listened to me. He was the best of critical friends. The book is dedicated to other – younger – members of our family.

INTRODUCTION
PRINCIPLES BEFORE POLITICS

In the spring of 1913 a number of female political activists set fire to several country houses, burned down a grand stand at Ayr racecourse and destroyed the walls and windows of a railway station by placing a home-made bomb in it. Telephone and telegraph wires were damaged in several districts: in Oldham sixty telephone wires were cut and communication with the north of England seriously disrupted. Thin test tubes filled with phosphorus, ink bottles without corks and corrosive acid were placed in pillar-boxes to destroy letters deposited in them. On one occasion a mail van containing mutilated post burst into flames. Flower beds were damaged, windows were broken and the glass of thirteen famous pictures in Manchester Art Gallery was shattered. Windsor Castle was closed to the public.

Emmeline Pankhurst (1858–1928) took responsibility for this outbreak of terrorism. One of the most fascinating, and indeed one of the most controversial, female figures of all time in British political history, she led an organisation committed to gaining the vote for women. The basic facts of her political life are widely known. In 1903, frustrated at the lack of progress achieved by the existing women's suffrage movement, she founded the Women's Social and Political Union (WSPU), which adopted a confrontational style of politics. Soon her organisation was notorious for its militant and violent actions. However, with the outbreak of war in August 1914, Emmeline suspended suffrage activities, worked hard for the war effort and was transformed into a popular heroine. After the war, partly as a reward for their war effort and partly as a result of pre-war suffrage activities, women achieved a limited vote.

For some people Emmeline Pankhurst is the emblem of the suffragette movement, a courageous and beautiful heroine who overcame the restrictions and prejudices of Victorian and Edwardian society to herald a new dawn of female equality. Moreover, her willingness to sacrifice her health, her financial security and ultimately her life for women's suffrage is admired and often romanticised. In contrast, others regard her campaign of violence as a direct assault upon the values inherent in womanhood; to them she is an abhorrence, a traitor to her sex and class for engaging in activities no sane women would have considered.

Certainly there is an ambiguity about Emmeline which defies easy characterisation and makes it difficult to label her since she often espoused contradictory politics. She appears to be a complex, paradoxical figure, and an idiosyncratic mixture of feminine charm and political guile. By nature a visionary and idealist who preferred novels to intellectual tomes, she was a skilled, practical and pragmatic politician. She championed unpopular causes, was notorious for her unorthodox politics yet was considered a 'true lady', genteel, softly spoken with impeccable dress sense and equally impeccable manners. At all times she maintained a professional façade of femininity while at the same time breaking every known standard of acceptable female conduct. Under her elegant exterior beat an iron determination. She may have been softly spoken, but Emmeline could also be breathtakingly intransigent and obstreperous. According to her erstwhile supporter, and later critic, Teresa Billington-Greig: 'Emmeline Pankhurst was a very wonderful woman, very beautiful, very gracious, very persuasive. ... She was a most astute statesman, a skilled politician, a self-dedicated re-shaper of the world – and a dictator without mercy.'[1]

Emphatically middle class, from a wealthy family and belonging to a political elite, she nonetheless championed the cause of the underdog. Mancunian by birth and by upbringing, she rarely identified with that city or the north of England, preferring Paris and Parisian chic. To the unsympathetic eye she appears a political dilettante. By upbringing a radical, she began her own political career as a Liberal, became enamoured of socialism, grew into an entrenched and militant feminist and ended up as Conservative parliamentary candidate for Whitechapel, a working-class area in the poorer section of London. Ironies abound. Her managerial style was incisive and allegedly autocratic, yet she worked to preserve democracy. As leader of the richest women's political organisation in history – which managed a successful and lucrative commercial enterprise as well as a suffrage campaign – her personal life was one long financial crisis characterised by business failures. With the outbreak of war in August 1914, Emmeline Pankhurst, at the height of her militant campaigns, suspended suffrage activities to support her old enemy Lloyd George in the war effort. During the First World War she adopted and persuaded others to adopt babies of single mothers, later evincing deep shock when her own daughter gave birth to a boy without being married. Initially a committed internationalist, she had by the end of her life rejected internationalism in favour of the British Empire. She made her reputation by demanding votes for women for greater social and economic justice, yet, once the vote was won, she used this achievement to campaign against Bolshevism in America and against the spread of venereal disease in Canada, both seen as examples of sexual immorality.

To marshal this inchoate life into an orderly narrative is a difficult task. Her long and eventful political career is not easily summed up, since her failings were no less manifest than her achievements. However, this biography will argue that even when Emmeline acted surprisingly, she did not necessarily act out of character. My aim is to examine the sequence and causation of her many changes and to make sense of the contradictions by arguing that her riveting blend of passion and politics was essentially focused on issues rather than on political parties. Emmeline Pankhurst, it will be argued, was a zealous, energetic, idiosyncratic, obsessive, progressive and pragmatic and 'free-floating' political individual, and remained so all her life. She may have been involved in a plethora of political movements and political parties but her commitment to certain big ideas remained constant. For there was more than a modicum of consistency in Emmeline's values, attitudes and behaviour. This book will demonstrate how she remained committed to parliamentary democracy and to women's rights throughout her political life and how she translated these fundamental values into guiding principles from which she never wavered. Emmeline was a woman who lived for the moment, a woman of improvisation who responded creatively to events rather than a coherent political strategist who planned each step ahead. She was a superb extempore speaker with colossal leadership skills who remained in the vanguard of politics throughout her life. Behind her gracefulness and charm was an extraordinarily retentive memory for political detail and a steely determination to win, whatever the cost to herself, her family and her friends. Many found it hard to reconcile her obvious beauty with intelligence, since women were either considered pretty and empty-headed, or clever and ugly. As *Saturday Night* observed before its reporter met her: 'I imagined a hatchet-faced old dame, with a hatchet in her belt, and her hat on an angle of forty-five degrees. In place of these I found a lady, singularly attractive in appearance, graceful in carriage, dignified in bearing, and a public speaker of culture as well as force'.[2] Her message, however, remained hard-hitting and uncompromising.

HISTORIOGRAPHY

Emmeline, her daughters and those who were acquainted with her wrote the first books about her life. Emmeline Pankhurst's *My Own Story* (1914)[3], Sylvia Pankhurst's *The Life of Emmeline Pankhurst* (1935)[4] and Christabel Pankhurst's *Unshackled: The Story of How We Won the Vote* (1959)[5] provide insights into the minds of the important leaders of women's suffrage. Rebecca West's brilliantly evocative essay 'A Reed of Steel' in *The Young Rebecca: Writings of Rebecca West, 1911–1917* (1933)[6] is an insightful sketch written by a novelist who knew the suffragette leader. Books published a few decades later provide a historical perspective but tend to be more critical, and sometimes disparaging, of Emmeline. Rupert Butler's *As They Saw Her ... Emmeline Pankhurst* (1970)[7], Harold Champion's *The True Book about Emmeline Pankhurst* (1963)[8], David Mitchell's *The Fighting Pankhursts* (1967)[9] and Martin Pugh's recently published *The Pankhursts* (2001)[10] are typical examples of this genre. Quite naturally, Emmeline Pankhurst's life has been included in the histories of women's suffrage. Roger Fulford's *Votes for Women* (1957),[11] which recounts the wider story of the suffragists as well as the suffragettes, and Andrew Rosen's scholarly narrative of the suffragette movement, *Rise up Women* (1974),[12] both tend to belittle her achievement. The birth and growth of feminist politics brought a new perspective to suffrage history and of Emmeline Pankhurst's role within it. One of the first books to break both new empirical and methodological ground is Jill Liddington and Jill Norris's *One Hand Tied Behind Us* (1978).[13] Yet these two feminist historians tend to be rather dismissive of the WSPU and their estimation of Emmeline Pankhurst is broadly negative. In contrast, she has been valorised as a major political icon by a number of contemporary feminists keen to establish a psychological and political link between present heroines and the past. Such feminists are drawn by the symbolism of the suffragette leader's challenge to male authority, while her later alleged jingoism and move to conservatism are relegated to the sidelines and viewed as unfortunate episodes in an otherwise unblemished political life. Indeed Martha Vicinus' *The Widening Sphere* (1972),[14] Jane Marcus's introduction to her collection of primary sources in *Suffrage and the Pankhursts* (1987)[15] and June Purvis's chapter in *Votes for Women* (2000)[16] portray Emmeline Pankhurst as a heroine fully committed to feminist ideals. Sandra Stanley Holton's essays are less adulatory and provide a fresh understanding of Emmeline's motivation.[17] Interestingly, although there have been many articles and chapters in books about Emmeline, there has been no full-length scholarly historical biography of her whole life.

The name Emmeline Pankhurst is synonymous with suffrage and historians have tended to focus on her suffragette activities. In doing so, they have ignored her other contributions to social and political reform.[18] Indeed, the historiographical lens is so tightly focused on the Edwardian suffragette period that other periods and campaigns have been neglected, with the result that her contribution as a wider social reformer has been diminished. Such a narrow focus has served to see women's political involvement in the early twentieth century as 'an isolated political pantomime ... a dynamic, yet brief, political intervention.'[19] This emphasis on such a short historical period, it is argued, undermines women's continuous struggle for equality since the beginning of the nineteenth century and beyond.

In a way, Emmeline has been the victim of a suffragette marketing success. No one could dispute the fact that her most famous contribution was to women's suffrage, but, in focusing on her time as suffragette leader, her contribution to other political campaigns has been underestimated. From her early girlhood until she died Emmeline was politically committed. This biography will therefore examine her life in the light of what Sandra Holton has called 'the previously neglected continuities' of the nineteenth and early twentieth centuries.[20] Her pre-suffrage, suffrage and post-suffrage experiences may not be a seamless continuity, but equally they were not as disjunctive as is sometimes stated. For

Emmeline Pankhurst suffrage was only ever a pathway to the ultimate goal of greater social and economic justice. She was in a continual state of political development, a woman who was engaged in a lifetime struggle to improve the lives of women. She helped to frame local politics in Manchester and was a political activist of some distinction before she founded her own organisation, the Women's Social and Political Union. Moreover, after the vote was won she did not fade into political obscurity and continued, as she had done in the days before the suffragette movement, to be involved in other forms of political and feminist campaigning.

This book will be primarily a political, rather than a personal, biography. Despite leading her life in the full glare of publicity, she remained an intensely private person. According to the composer Ethel Smyth, at one time a close friend, 'no one can ever have had a profounder sense of personal dignity ... one aspect of it was an almost morbid delicacy about everything that touched her private life'.[21] She even objected to the way in which she was known as Mrs Emmeline Pankhurst in America; in England, she stated, she was always known simply as 'Mrs Pankhurst' and the 'dragging in' of her first name was something that she found intrusive. She insisted that, in England, 'we consider one's first name as one's personal property'[22] – people of her generation were usually addressed by their second name by all save family and intimate friends. 'I am very British' she once wrote to Elizabeth Robins; 'I fear and feel very dumb and stupid when called upon to show my personal feelings in public.'[23] In Emmeline Pankhurst's view, the personal had no place in the political sphere. She was, according to a WSPU member, an idea rather than a friend, a fanatical torchbearer rather than a mother, a consummate political activist rather than a playmate. Certainly, her relationships with women remain one of the enigmas of the suffrage years. She appeared to have few intimate relationships except with her daughters, especially Christabel, and with those who worked with her in the suffrage and other movements. Emmeline Pankhurst was not given to self-analysis in public; neither do her political speeches tell anything of her personal life. She left no diary, and the archives reveal a complete absence of the kind of personal revelation which deals with private – that is to say affective or sexual – matters.

It is a truism that leaders often have an outer existence markedly different from their private self – which is another way of saying that those in the public eye are generally dishonest and have secret sexual lives to hide. In a recent article in *The Times* Martin Pugh claimed that Emmeline was a lesbian, presumably engaging in a full-blown love affair with Ethel Smyth, a well-known sapphist. In *Female Pipings in Eden* Ethel Smyth talks of 'staring at her with the cool, critical eye of one not yet in love' – which might suggest that they enjoyed a stronger emotional and sexual relationship at some later time. But while the two women certainly shared a bedroom from time to time, the modern obsession with the sexuality of the famous is not one that Emmeline would have condoned. If she did have romantic or sexual liaisons either before or after her husband's death, they were kept well hidden. Passionate same-sex affection was viewed as acceptable, and certainly emotional attachment can and does exist without sex. It is the modern obsession with sex which gives rise to the interest in her sexual preferences rather than any act on her part. Any reluctance she may have had to speak about personal affairs would certainly have been due, in part, to emotional shyness, but she would no doubt have been careful to protect herself against the antagonism faced by lesbians at that time. 'It is difficult for me to express feeling of any kind,' she wrote, claiming that it was only through work that her 'natural reticence and diffidence' had been overcome. Indeed, she once asked Elizabeth Robins to publicise her own and Christabel's work and tell the public what they were really like.[24] The fact that this did not include any reference to lesbianism is unimportant. What is true is that Emmeline Pankhurst developed a feminist consciousness and remained true to feminist values and to women's issues for the whole of her life. In that special sense she was a woman-identified woman, which some radical feminists would term 'lesbian'.

Of course, piecing together the life of a woman who left no diary, letters or personal collections is somewhat challenging. This is especially so when even the basic facts of her life are difficult to establish, thus making it hard for the biographer to distinguish myth from reality. Emmeline was registered *Emiline* at birth but in adult life obviously preferred the revised spelling of her name. Her mother's surname has been variously identified as Jane Quine or Jane Craine. (It appears as Craine on Emmeline's birth certificate – the confusion probably arising because her grandmother's maiden name was Quine before she subsequently married William Craine.) Today Emmeline is sometimes confused in the popular mind with Emily Wilding Davison, who on June 4th 1913, in an attempt to gain publicity for women's suffrage, ran out on to the Derby racecourse and died a few days later from injuries sustained when the king's horse knocked her down. In an article published in *The Observer*, Barbara Ellen, critical of modern women for their obsession with marriage, asked: 'Did Emmeline Pankhurst get trampled under the King's horse for *this?*'[25] The *Daily Telegraph*, in a recent cartoon strip intended for young readers, called her Emily Pankhurst rather than Emmeline.

The life of a person with broad interests whose political life crossed various historical eras, themes and topics further challenges the biographer's reservoir of knowledge and understanding. Emmeline Pankhurst was born a Victorian and lived through to the beginning of the modern era; she was involved in a number of social reforms, in the Poor Law, and in education; she was active in the Labour, Liberal and Conservative parties; she worked hard for the war effort in the First World War; she campaigned for Social Purity; she was an activist not only in contemporary local politics but also in American and Canadian politics; and, above all, she was deeply and continuously committed to women's suffrage. The historian, who can never hope to become an expert in all of these fields, engages with many of them at her peril.

THEMES AND CONTENT

The biography is structured chronologically but within this chronology themes will be identified and examined so that an analysis – rather than a mere description – of Emmeline Pankhurst's political life can emerge. Emmeline was the eldest daughter of a wealthy Manchester manufacturer, Robert Goulden, and his wife, Sophia. Both of her parents were committed to social reform and encouraged their sons and daughters to become involved in various political activities. It will be argued that Emmeline's radical heritage played a significant part in shaping her future beliefs. In these crucial formative years the seeds of her commitment to suffrage and to women's issues germinated, along with her taste for theatricality and her lasting tendency to take partisan positions which were typically pro-French and anti-German.

In 1879 Emmeline Goulden married the much older radical barrister and politician Richard Pankhurst. At the same time as being a – more-

or-less – conventional wife and mother of five children, she was engaged in politics both on her husband's behalf and in support of her own beliefs. For long before she became involved in suffrage, she was well known as a political activist in her local community. This was her training ground – here she took the opportunity to practise the organisational and speaking skills which were to become the hallmark of her leadership. During this period she shifted her allegiance from the Liberal Party to the newly emerging Independent Labour Party (ILP), a shift that was less about ideology than about political practice. Emmeline represented the Independent Labour Party as a Poor Law Guardian in working-class districts of Manchester – and made a name for herself through her work in improving workhouse conditions, particularly for women, children and the elderly, and in challenging the economic parsimony of the local government. When the family moved temporarily to London, she co-founded her first suffrage organisation, the Women's Franchise League (WFrL), and set about developing the style and politics which would later characterise the Women's Social and Political Union.

When Richard died of a perforated stomach ulcer in 1898, it put an end to a good marriage, a political partnership and a modicum of financial stability. Richard, forever defending lost causes, left little money to his widow and four surviving children, so she was forced to seek paid work. Now aged 40 and no longer in the shadow of her famous husband, she was to make the Pankhurst name internationally famous. Once widowed, Emmeline took paid employment as Registrar of Births and Deaths in Rusholme, a working-class district in Manchester, remaining in this post until 1907. The book will examine how it was that someone like Emmeline Pankhurst, utterly provincial and from a relatively obscure political backwater with no obvious social advantages, could have become such a powerful national figure.

In 1903 she founded her very own organisation, the Women's Social and Political Union (WSPU), at her house in Manchester. As an organisation, the WSPU was based on the charisma of its leader rather than on constitutional procedures. At first, it mirrored the peaceful and legitimate measures of other protest groups: it organised public meetings and demonstrations, wrote propaganda literature, lobbied MPs and petitioned Parliament. Throughout this period, Emmeline continued her involvement in radical politics, but gradually became disillusioned with the ILP. Even though she eventually left the party, she remained rooted to socialist and radical traditions during this period. Her socialist ideals meant that she never regarded votes for women as an end in itself; for her it was always the means by which social and economic justice for women would be achieved. Nevertheless, mindful of past defeats, she refused to let her organisation become yet another suffrage organisation which failed. When peaceful methods proved to be ineffective, and with the move of WSPU headquarters to London, she adopted a more confrontational style of politics. Spurred on by the death of her son, her mother and her sister, Emmeline directed her anger and grief against all those who opposed votes for women. As the WSPU membership grew more combative (prompted by her pronouncements about militancy), as Deeds replaced Words, so Emmeline showed she would brook no dissent from the members of the WSPU. Those who disagreed with her policies were forced to leave.

Suffragettes chained themselves to railings, wrote 'Votes for Women' in acid on golf courses, disrupted the postal service, broke windows and burnt down empty buildings. Not surprisingly, government reaction to the violence was negative. Emmeline was arrested, charged and convicted: altogether she was imprisoned fourteen times. In 1912 she went on her first hunger strike. By 1914, according to her doctor, 'Mrs Pankhurst has lost almost a stone in weight. She suffered greatly from nausea and gastric disturbances, and was released in a toxic condition with a high temperature and a very intermittent pulse. She is nervously shocked by all she has gone through, and is unable to sleep properly, her rest being disturbed by dreams and by neuralgic pains.'[26] Her life was now in danger, yet Emmeline continued to advocate violent action. Her contribution to the increasing militancy of the WSPU will be examined and it will be suggested that, although ordinary WSPU members often initiated militant actions, the suffragette leader encouraged their escalation. The book will also determine to what extent she was a skilful political pragmatist or whether she was merely, as some historians suggest, an overbearing autocrat.

Militancy may have dominated the life and indeed the histories of Emmeline Pankhurst, but throughout even the most violent episodes of WSPU militancy she, and her organisation, still pursued traditional methods of lobbying support for the vote. And not only during times of truce. While fronting a paramilitary campaign of terror, Emmeline continued to tour Britain to publicise votes for women, organising meetings, deputations, demonstrations, exhibitions and other legal forms of protest. During this period, she becomes increasingly dedicated to challenging inequalities of gender rather than of class. But despite this – and despite now mixing with the social elite – she never relinquished her commitment to working-class women.

At a time when travelling outside Europe was both time-consuming and punitively expensive, Emmeline visited the USA three times – in 1909, in 1911 and in 1913. Her visits were intended primarily to raise money for herself and for the WSPU, but also to publicise the cause of women's suffrage in Britain. From her lectures, she came across as a committed democrat who believed in extending the franchise to all women regardless of race, colour or creed. She also visited Canada twice in 1909 and 1911. The Canadian suffrage movement, with its different historical tradition, methods, and ideological principles, gave her a surprisingly generous welcome and a moderate degree of acceptance.

In August 1914 suffragette activity suddenly stopped as Britain prepared for war against Germany. Emmeline decided that there was no point in continuing to fight for the vote when there might be no country to vote in and therefore placed the WSPU, and its funds, at the disposal of the government. She called for military conscription for men, industrial conscription for women and the abolition of trade unions. The book will investigate why suffragette activity was abandoned as soon as the war began and will suggest that her brand of patriotism reflected a radical, as well as a conservative, outlook. It will go on to examine the reasons why she supported the war, and argue that these were linked to her childhood experiences and to her deep-seated political values and convictions rather than simply to nationalist fervour. During the war, Emmeline was transformed from an arch enemy of the Liberals to one of its most effective advocates. As an official representative of HM Government, she toured Russia, America and Canada, raising funds for Serbia and encouraging the war effort. The war was a turning point for her in that she abandoned her previous commitment to socialism and internationalism in favour of a new reconfiguration of the British Empire.

After the war, women over the age of 30 were given the vote, yet Emmeline did not lose her political momentum. On the contrary, she became involved in a wide variety of issues: lecturing in America on the perils of Bolshevism, leading a campaign against venereal disease in Canada, then returning to stand as Conservative parliamentary candidate for Whitechapel. These last *volte-face* – as it appears – have provided the grounds for labelling her a reactionary. But any such neat categorisation risks missing the point about her both on a personal and on an ideological basis. If she did indeed become a Tory, she was a mightily anarchic one, uncomfortable in the shires and preferring to act out her new political allegiances in the working-class districts of London. Her childhood experiences, family background, her early political life and her suffrage years continued to shape her political actions.

Born in 1858, she died in 1928 and occupied a special vantage point, both looking back to the Victorian age and forward to the special challenges of the first quarter of the twentieth century. The book will seek to underline the unchanging convictions which created consistency in Emmeline's political life. It will make a qualitative assessment of her contribution to various radical, and indeed conservative, causes and will summarise her development as a political activist from her early experiences in Manchester to her leadership of the largest militant suffrage organisation in the history of the British Isles.

Part I

A POLITICAL APPRENTICESHIP 1858–1903

1

SHAPING A LIFE 1858–80

FAMILY BACKGROUND

Emmeline was born on July 15th 1858, a hot summer's day in which temperatures reached an extraordinarily un-British and swelteringly high 85°F.[1] As with most things surrounding her life, even this has become a matter of dispute since she, her daughters and most of her biographers would have it that she was born on July 14th. Of course, one day's difference in celebrating a birthday is generally of no consequence but with Emmeline it had significance in its association with Bastille Day. On July 14th 1789 revolutionaries had attacked the Bastille, a state prison whose high and massive walls were the embodiment of autocracy and repression. The storming of the Bastille had heralded a new age of freedom, justice and humanity, and Bastille Day became hugely symbolic to radicals like Emmeline. In later life, she was to use the symbol to great effect in her likening of the suffragette struggle against an intransigent government with the French revolutionaries' fights against tyranny. In 1909, when presented with a replica medal struck to commemorate the winning of the Bastille, she announced that she had always been proud of the fact that she had been born on July 14th. She 'had always thought that the knowledge that her birthday had been the anniversary of the final taking of that monument of tyranny had had an influence upon her whole life.'[2] In creating her own birthday, she had also forged an image of herself as a natural revolutionary.

And today, each year on July 14th sympathisers and family congregate around her statue at Westminster to commemorate her birthday and to honour her memory.

Emmeline was born at home in Swan Street, Moss Side, Manchester, into a middle-class radical family. She was the eldest daughter of a wealthy Manchester calico manufacturer, Robert Goulden, and his wife, Sophia Jane Craine.[3]

There were strong Manx connections. Emmeline Goulden's mother was born in Lonan, Isle of Man, in 1833, a member of an old-established family that could trace its ancestry back to the early fifteenth century. The name originated from MacCiarain and was of Scottish origin. Some of her ancestors had clearly been in trouble with the authorities: in 1422 Donald McCraine was tried for baiting the Lieutenant Governor's men in Kirk Michael, and in 1658 William Craine was sentenced to have his ears cut off and fined £10 for slander.[4] However, the later Craines, reputable yeomen, were well respected on the island and not really given to radical politics. Although it is often stated that Emmeline's mother was the daughter of a Manx farmer, this was not the case. In fact, Sophia Jane's father, William Craine, was a shoemaker by trade, who subsequently took over and managed a boarding house with his wife, also called Jane, first at North Quay and then later at Christian Road, Douglas, on the Isle of Man.

Manx inhabitants, proud of their radical heritage, claim that Emmeline's militancy should be attributed – in part – to her Manx blood. Speaking years later to an American audience, she herself stated that the suffrage idea came naturally to her since her mother had enjoyed the franchise in her own country.[5] The Isle of Man was (and still is) independent from Britain with its own parliament and the right to formulate its own domestic policies. Manx women enjoyed superior legal and political rights and participated more fully in public life than

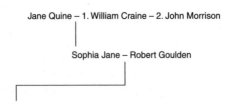

Jane Quine – 1. William Craine – 2. John Morrison

Sophia Jane – Robert Goulden

Walter, Emmeline, Edmund, Mary Jane, Herbert, Robert, Harold, Eva, Effie, Ada

English women. It is said that one key event in Manx history precipitated this: in 1098 two rival chieftains, one from the north of the island and one from the south, fought for supremacy at a place called Santwat. After a long and bloody battle the northern chieftain won – allegedly because the northern women had turned out in force to help their menfolk on the battlefield. But the Isle of Man was always a strong sea-faring nation and women were used to being left alone to manage domestic and political affairs. Moreover, there was a powerful Gaelic tradition in the island which encouraged women to take a full part in public life, and the religious ethos of Methodism, which was strong in the island, accorded women a greater role in the church than most other religions.

More importantly, and as a consequence of their political, religious and cultural heritage, Manx single and propertied women gained the vote in 1881, thirty-seven years before their English counterparts – the first country in the world to grant the vote to women. Of course, this radical reform was neither a foregone conclusion nor an historical accident but the result of a combination of tradition, Manx pride and the effects of campaigning by suffragists. The House of Keys, the Isle of Man equivalent of the House of Commons, was elected for the first time in 1866 so voting was new to all of the electorate. Since it was a small community, the Isle of Man had a significantly more personalised system of voting and was less dependent on political parties than the mainland. (In Britain at the time the two main parties – the Liberals and Conservatives – were against votes for women for different reasons. The Conservatives in general were ideologically opposed to any extension of democracy, while the Liberals feared that a limited franchise would benefit the Conservatives too much.) On the Isle of Man not only was each candidate well known but each voter was too; there would be no political surprises if women were enfranchised.

A proposed Isle of Man Suffrage Bill (1880) attracted the attention of the Manchester National Society for Women's Suffrage, which took a keen interest in these issues, and, in turn, provided an impetus for the local movement. In 1880 Lydia Becker and Mrs Alice Scatcherd, friends of Emmeline's parents and of her future husband Richard Pankhurst, visited the island to address a number of meetings. These meetings were described as 'crowded', 'large and influential' and attended by 'ladies of the better class'.[6] Manx suffragists and their supporters adopted the tactics of the Manchester campaigners by holding meetings, obtaining favourable press coverage, signing petitions and questioning candidates about their views on female suffrage. At a large public meeting on November 1st 1880, in which various members of the House of Keys were present, a resolution was passed unanimously that the franchise be extended to women. On November 3rd, just as the House of Keys was preparing to consider the suffrage bill, an editorial in one of the island's chief newspapers, *Mona's Herald*, called for the inclusion of women electors on the grounds that there should be no taxation without representation. And so on November 5th 1881, when the House of Keys debated the issue, there were few arguments against votes for women and the motion was carried by 16 votes to 3. Over 700 women, consisting of between 5 and 10 per cent of the electorate, were enfranchised by this measure. Women's suffrage had arrived, paradoxically, on the Isle of Man. Neither Emmeline Pankhurst nor her mother were directly involved in the campaign but when, in 1981, the Isle of Man Post Office Authority issued a stamp to commemorate the centenary of Island women being given the vote, both Emmeline Pankhurst and Sophia Jane Goulden were featured prominently.

Sophia Jane met and married Robert Goulden, a young man from Manchester, England. In her youth, Sophia Jane Craine had been an 'unusually good-looking young lady' with a 'bright and attractive personality.'[7] Robert most probably fell in love with his future wife while lodging with the Craine family. The Isle of Man was a popular resort for northern factory workers who flocked to its many lodging houses for their annual holiday, and Robert may have been one of them. Equally, he may have visited the island to sell his calico to sail makers.[8] Robert and Sophia Jane married on September 8th 1853 at the romantic setting of Kirk Braddan Church on the Isle of Man. She was 18 and he was 24.

There is a mystery surrounding Emmeline's father's family background. It is sometimes believed that Robert Goulden was from an Irish background. It is equally conceivable that Robert Goulden, although baptised, may have been of Jewish origin. Traditional rabbinical scholars maintain that the Gouldens of Manchester were Jewish, but there is no trace of Robert in remaining records. Robert Goulden's parents were certainly from a humble background. His mother had been a fustian cutter while his father had been press-ganged into the navy. Emmeline's paternal roots were equally radical. Her grandmother was active in the Anti-Corn Law League and her grandfather narrowly escaped injury at a franchise demonstration in St Peter's Fields, Manchester, where an unarmed crowd of about 80,000 men, women and children were attacked by the cavalry. This unprovoked and brutal attack – 11 people were killed and over 400 injured – shocked the public. The event, quickly dubbed 'Peterloo', popularised suffrage reform and gave an heroically romantic status to people like Emmeline's grandfather.

Robert and Sophia Goulden had six sons and five daughters.[9] The eldest son of the family died when he was 2½ years old but ten survived: Walter, Emmeline (later Pankhurst), Edmund, Mary (later Clarke), Herbert, Effie (later Bailey), Robert, Ada Sophia (later Bach), Alfred Harold, and Eva Gertrude (later Brown). Robert Goulden was a self-made man. At the time of his wedding he was a mere errand boy,[10] but he later graduated to become a manufacturer, first in partnership and finally as managing director of his own business. Later in his life he entered into a further partnership with Mr John Hody James and between 1867 and 1887 the two men managed the Seedley Printworks. It would appear that Robert Goulden was very much the junior partner, for whereas Hody James lived in Seedley House, a large mansion standing in its own grounds, the Gouldens lived in Seedley Cottage, an altogether more modest accommodation.

The house in Seedley in which Emmeline lived for most of her childhood was surrounded by countryside and the district was one of the most secluded and desirable areas within the suburbs of Manchester.[11] Indeed, Seedley was the prime residential location for a large section of the business community of Manchester and boasted many city dignitaries amongst its inhabitants. However, by the end of the nineteenth century Seedley had changed out of recognition: the combined expansion of Salford and Manchester more than doubled the number of dwellings. Such rapid expansion meant that the new houses were smaller, designed to appeal to the tastes and the pockets of artisans and workers rather than to the rich business classes. The new streets surrounding Seedley Printworks were named in honour of the Arctic explorer Nansen and included Greenland, Iceland and Norway Streets – the district was commonly known as the 'North Pole'. One street name, oddly out of place, was Goulden Street, established to commemorate Robert's contribution to the local community.

The Goulden family typically spent their holidays at 9 Strathallan Crescent, a rather charming white stuccoed building on the sea-front of

Douglas Bay, Isle of Man, which was owned by Emmeline's step-grand-father. Her grandfather, William Craine, had died in 1866 and in 1874 her grandmother re-married at St Tomas's Church, Douglas; her second husband was a mariner called John Morrison. In 1878 the house was bought by Emmeline's father and was used as a holiday home. In 1892 Emmeline's father died, and her mother left Manchester and returned to the Isle of Man to live at the house for another 40 years. There is photo-graphic and oral evidence to suggest that Emmeline Pankhurst, and her children, continued to visit the Isle of Man. The historian Patricia de Ban remembers her own father meeting Christabel Pankhurst there, and Richard Pankhurst recalls his mother, Sylvia, talking about her visits to the Isle of Man.[12]

Her parents throughout her early childhood undoubtedly fostered Emmeline's theatricality, her commitment to suffrage and her emanci-patory politics. Both of her parents were committed to social reform, so much so that, even as a young girl, Emmeline was exposed to radical politics and taken to meet the foremost intellectuals of the time. Her parents were members of Manchester's radical elite, which meant that she was surrounded in her childhood by left-wing intelligentsia includ-ing Jacob and Ursula Bright, Elizabeth Wolstenholme-Elmy … and, of course, her future husband Richard Pankhurst. While it is often assumed that it was Richard Pankhurst who formed Emmeline's poli-tics, proper credit must be given to the oblique influence of her parents, to her early childhood and to her later education – both formal and informal – in Paris for shaping her radical beliefs.

Emmeline's father took a keen interest in public matters. For five or six years he was Liberal representative for the Seedley Ward on Salford Town Council. One of his obituary notices affirmed that, although he was a favourite with the working class, he also took part in several agita-tions for the benefit of the ratepayers of Salford. A strong supporter of Cobden and Bright, Robert Goulden was especially active on the Council at the time of the cotton famine. During the American Civil War between 1860 and 1865 he helped to sustain the neutrality of Britain and campaigned for the emancipation of the slaves. When Henry Ward Beecher visited Britain in 1863 to promote American Union, Robert Goulden was appointed to the Welcoming Committee and read the address that Henry Beecher was asked to present to Abraham Lincoln on his return.[13] Emmeline was introduced to these emancipatory politics at an early age. She recalled having been mesmerised by Harriet Beecher Stowe's famous novel *Uncle Tom's Cabin*, which was read to her as a bedtime story by her mother. (Harriet Beecher Stowe was Henry Ward Beecher's sister.) This powerful melodramatic novel, although subjected to heavy criticism by twentieth-century readers, was extremely popular during Emmeline's childhood. It revealed the sufferings caused by slavery by describing how the hero of the story, the uncomplaining and pious Uncle Tom, was sold to a brutal cotton plantation owner who finally beat him to death. Her parents not only read such improving stories to their daughter but they encouraged her to do something practical about the injustices that touched her compassion. Theirs was a doctrine of Deeds as well as Words. Before long, young Emmeline set about raising money to relieve the poverty of the emancipated slaves.

Robert Goulden was a political activist who enjoyed the lighter side of life; he was no tortured, dreary politician with an unhealthy dislike of entertainment. On the contrary, he was a promoter of the Manchester Athenaeum, a member of the Dramatic Reading Society and considered a 'fine elocutionist with much dramatic power'.[14] At one time he purchased the Prince of Wales Theatre in Salford for use as a concert hall but in 1882 transferred the building to his son Edmund to use as a theatre.[15] Under Edmund's management the theatre's repertory featured an unusually heavy emphasis on Victorian melodrama and became known locally as the 'blood tin'. Blood-curdling plays like 'Murder in the Red Barn' and 'The Face at the Window' were performed, as well as the popular drama 'From Mill Street to Mansion' in which the mill owner's son entices the local mill girl to come with him to his strangely isolated mansion.[16] There is no doubt that Emmeline inherited her considerable dramatic flair from her father – she loved the theatre and visited it whenever she had time to do so.[17]

EARLY POLITICAL INFLUENCES

Emmeline's early views on Irish politics were formed in her childhood. In her autobiography she recalled being affected by the Fenian Revolt in Ireland and the subsequent reaction of the British government towards it. In 1867, when she was under 10 years of age, the leaders of the Fenian rebellion had killed a police officer while trying to escape from a prison van. Three of the leaders, Allen, O'Brien and Larkin, were hanged publicly for murder in Manchester. Emmeline remembered passing the prison on the way home from school and witnessing the remains of the gallows through a gap in the wall. Shaken by this experience, she later identified it as a formative influence. Indeed many of her political views, and in particular her suffragette activities, were affected and shaped by her awareness of Irish politics.

In her autobiography, Emmeline also states that: 'I had always been an unconscious suffragist. With my temperament and my surroundings I could scarcely have been otherwise.'[18] Her mother first introduced her to women's suffrage. The suffrage movement in Manchester was very active in the 1870s and her mother, although not a subscriber to the Manchester suffrage society, was obviously sympathetic, ordering the *Women's Suffrage Journal* each week.[19] Emmeline, now aged 15, was taken to the first-ever suffrage meeting that was held at the Free Trade Hall in February 1874. She would have recognised her parents' friends on the platform: Jacob Bright chaired the meeting and Lydia Becker, Rhoda Garrett, Miss Ashworth and Miss Sturge were the main speakers. In terms of audience numbers, it was a huge success and the hall was full. Unfortunately, according to the *Manchester Critic*, the women speakers were too inexperienced to be very effective. With the exception of Lydia Becker, their voices could not be heard at the back of the hall; hecklers kept singing Rule Britannia, and different speakers repeated many of the same points.[20] Notwithstanding this, Lydia Becker made a forceful impression on the young Emmeline – even though she later admitted that she had not fully understood the points being made. Many years later she went out of her way to acknowledge her mother's influence upon her political development. In 1909 she told a newspaper reporter: 'My mother is our greatest sympathiser. She is an old lady over 80 and she has gone back to live in the Isle of Man. She is proud of what we are all doing. There is no one in England who watches for the papers more eagerly than she to see what is the latest news from the suffragettes.'[21]

At first, Emmeline was educated at a Manchester boarding school, returning home at the weekends – but she did not enjoy the experience and certainly did not benefit from it. At this time in Britain educational provision for middle-class girls was generally of poor quality. The majority of girls did not attend school but were taught at home by their mothers, fathers or other relatives. Governesses, with varying success, educated a few. Sometimes the daughters of wealthy parents, as with Emmeline, were privately educated at day schools and sometimes boarding schools. At the end of a more or less expensive education they were able to play a few tunes on the piano, to sing, to dance the minuet, to draw a simple sketch, to sew a delicate sampler and sometimes to speak a little French. These accomplishments helped them achieve the Victorian ideal of the perfectly educated woman: a decorative, poised and empty-headed companion for a future husband. The low academic standard of such schools prompted one feminist to remark that girls were taught the three Ss rather than the three Rs: singing, sewing and simpering. A number of pioneering schools, often run by Unitarians, emphasised academic rather than domestic achievement but for the most part education was curiously detached from academic excellence.

In 1872, at the age of 14, she was sent to France to be educated at the École Normale in the Avenue de Neuilly, Paris, one of the pioneer institutions for the higher education of girls. The head of the school was Mlle Marchef-Girard, a distinguished educationalist who was later to become government inspector of schools in France. A play about her experiences at the school captures something of her obsession with appearance, her emotional intensity and her emerging political fervour. 'Emmeline is ushered into her bedroom at the École Normale. A manservant brings up her baggage. The room is bright and furnished with severe plainness, two beds, two chests of drawers, two dressing tables, two wash stands, two chairs. Emmeline seats herself. She feels tired and lonely. She leans against the bed, buries her head on her folded arms and weeps.' Emmeline apparently quickly recovers when Noémie Rochefort, 'a tall slim young girl with golden hair, three or four years older than Emmeline enters and sees her crying.' There is mutual admiration of their good looks – Noémie raves about Emmeline's beauty: 'But you are beautiful! The raven hair, the beautiful black eye-brows so finely arched, and those large eyes of violet blue, the olive skin .... What a beautiful throat .... You are svelte ... your lips are ravishing .... Will you be my friend? I adore you. We are to share this room. So we must be friends.' [22]

The principal of the school, committed to equal educational opportunities, constructed a curriculum which included chemistry, sciences and book-keeping as well as the usual accomplishments regarded as

essential for young middle-class women of the period. Although Noémie
Rochefort came from a patrician family, her parents, like Emmeline's,
were radicals. Noémie's aristocratic father was a leader of the Paris
Commune so the two, not surprisingly, became firm friends. Emmeline
deepened her love of France and developed a fierce animosity towards
Germany when, in 1870, after the bitter siege of Paris during which the
starving populace were forced to eat rats, France suffered a humiliating
defeat by the newly emerging German state. France was forced to surrender Alsace and Lorraine, areas rich in iron ore and agricultural land,
and to pay a war indemnity of five million francs. *Départements* were to
remain under German occupation until the price had been paid. To add
insult to an appalling injury, the new German Empire was proclaimed
in the Hall of Mirrors at Versailles. The left wing, critical that the
authorities had sold the birthright of their nation to a foreign invader
and fearful of a return to the *ancien régime*, refused to accept this punitive
treaty and rebelled against the decision of their more conciliatory leaders. Instead, they formed their own municipal government – the
Commune – to resist both the Germans and those who had succumbed
to its invasion. As the Germans looked on, the French armed forces bru-
tally crushed this nascent rebellion.

In Emmeline's play, the young women talk about Noémie's father, a
leader of the Paris Commune, who 'resigned from the National Assembly
rather than assent to the surrender of our two sister provinces, Alsace and
Lorraine. He is too great a patriot, too true a son of France ever to bow to
the Germans .... You will see them marching with their odious goosestep
through our beloved Paris. Oh their brutal heavy jaws and those cold
prominent eyes, cold and hard as the eyes of a snake, damn Prussian sav-
ages. They trample over the rights of all with their jackboots. Our Paris
occupied by those monsters.' This impassioned extract, heightened no
doubt for the sake of drama, nevertheless signals a key dimension within
her own emerging set of values – one that would come to affect some of
her future beliefs and actions. In Paris she also discovered Thomas
Carlyle's *History of the French Revolution* – it was to become a favourite
book. Paris's sense of history, the romanticism of the 1871 Paris
Commune and the experiences of her new friend coloured the imagina-
tion of Emmeline, who gloried in visions of resistance to unjust authority.

Emmeline remained at her Parisian school until she was 19 years old.
During this time, as with so many other women of her class and time,

she learned to speak French fluently. According to her daughter Sylvia, she fell in love with French 'dress, cooking, hotels and railways, French women, the French language and literature, anything and everything French were the best in the world'.[23] Even her favourite heroine, Joan of Arc, and her preferred song, the *Marseillaise*, were French. She remained a friend with Noémie after her schooling ended – Noémie married a Swiss painter – and returned to France when her sister Mary enrolled at her old school. During one visit she accepted a proposal of marriage from a French suitor who withdrew his suit quickly enough when her father refused a dowry. Shortly afterwards she agreed to marry Richard Pankhurst.

RICHARD PANKHURST

Just a few days before Christmas, on December 18th 1879, Emmeline Goulden aged 21 married Richard Pankhurst at St Lukes Weaste in the Parish of Eccles, Lancashire. He was 23 years older and only six years younger than her father. Emmeline's father, her sister Mary, H.E. Graham, John Cavanagh, Elizabeth Mary Casard and Esther Lightbown (whose relative Henry Lightbown was a radical and chair of the Seedley Workingmen's Liberal Association)[24] served as witnesses at the wedding. It was a sublime political union: Harriot Stanton Blatch, an American friend and political colleague, said of the marriage: 'She had smoldering fire, he kindled the flame.'

Richard Pankhurst was, in many ways, an ideal husband for Emmeline: he was a middle-class radical idealist committed to social reform and women's rights. The son of Henry Francis Pankhurst and Margaret Marsden, he was educated at the Manchester Grammar School and afterwards at Owens College, Manchester. In 1858, the year Emmeline was born, her future husband had graduated with a BA from the University of London. He gained his LLB in 1859 and his LLD in the year following. When Emmeline was just nine years old, Richard was already making a name for himself in the radical political circles of Manchester. By the mid-1860s, while still a young barrister, he had gained a formidable reputation for his work in educational and social reform and for his passionate commitment to women's rights. Between 1863 and 1876 he was the Honorary Secretary of the Union of Lancashire and Cheshire Mechanics' Institutes, promoted working-class education and was active in Sunday schools. In 1873 he was a candidate for membership of the Manchester School Board.

Certainly, he was an early and strong supporter of legislative reform for women on all matters from property to suffrage. He drafted the 1868 (unsuccessful) Married Women's Property Bill to enable women to have some control of their money after marriage and remained an influential member of the Married Women's Property Committee until his death. Richard Pankhurst was committed to women's suffrage long before he met Emmeline; for years he worked with Lydia Becker to promote the Cause, writing articles and giving lectures in its support, and was an extremely active member of the Manchester National Society for Women's Suffrage. In 1867 he helped organise a campaign to get women's names on the electoral register – 92 per cent of women in Manchester sent in claims. When this plan failed, he took the case to the Court of Common Pleas (Chorlton vs Lings and Chorlton vs Kessler), where he defended over 5,000 Manchester women who claimed the right to vote. He lost. Undeterred, in 1869 he wrote the successful amendment to the Municipal Corporations Bill (local government reform) which gave women the right to vote in municipal elections. Inspired and heartened by this, he set to work drafting the 1870 Women's Enfranchisement Bill to be introduced in the House of Commons by the radical MP Jacob Bright, brother of the more famous John. The bill would have allowed women to vote on the same terms as men – but, of course, it never became law.

At first, Emmeline rejected the notion of marriage to Richard and proposed instead that they should live together in a spirit of 'free union'. This was a bold and principled proposal which would undoubtedly have given offence in the wider middle-class society; women who chose to live 'in sin' were often subjected to harsh criticism even from other suffragists and radicals. However, feminists like Emmeline were often hostile to marriage – they considered it an unjust institution which placed women in a subordinate position, eroded their rights and subjected them to restrictions not applicable to single women. Marriage, in their view, was 'civil death' as well as death to any equal partnership. But Emmeline's opposition to wedlock was short-lived. Once married, Emmeline submitted to the laws of the land with the majority of her sex: she forfeited her last name; she did not enjoy the same rights to her own property and earnings as single women; and her husband was legally entitled to lock her up and rape her if he so wished. Any future children of the Pankhurst marriage would legally belong to Richard, who could, if he was disposed to do so, bar Emmeline access to them. When it came to being sexually faithful in marriage, there was one law for men, another quite different for women. If Richard was unfaithful, he might have been excused, but if Emmeline dared to commit adultery, it would have been considered unforgivable. Moreover, if Emmeline ever wished to leave her husband, she could not do so easily. Richard could seek divorce if his wife ever committed adultery, but she would have to claim bestiality, sodomy and other indignities, if she ever wanted to divorce him. Fortunately, in spite of these legal inequalities, the marriage was a happy one.

CONCLUSION

It would be easy to assume that the intellectual and physically unattractive Richard was all 'head', while the sensitive and rather glamorous Emmeline was all 'heart'. Easy, too, to assume that Emmeline Pankhurst, young, inexperienced and impressionable, was led to political maturity by her older, urbane and accomplished husband. But such assumptions would be misleading. Indeed, Emmeline's parents had encouraged their eldest daughter to develop a robust political and social consciousness of her own. She was immersed in political life at a very early age: her commitment to suffrage, her obsession with the Irish question, her theatricality, her support for slave emancipation, her Francophilism, her animosity towards an aggressive and imperialistic Germany were all formed when she was young and remained at the very core of her political thinking throughout her life. Indeed, her reluctance to marry Richard Pankhurst in favour of a free union was consistent with the radical and feminist politics of the time and hardly the action of a conventional empty-headed young woman bent on securing marriage to a famous Mancunian figure. Throughout the nineteen years of the marriage, theirs was as much a political as a personal partnership. In this matter of partnership Emmeline was indeed blessed with good fortune. Her marriage to Richard combined most favourably with the radical influence she had received from her parents to give her the best possible preparation for the epic struggle that was to follow – the struggle to win the vote.

Emmeline was also blessed with a ceaselessly energetic disposition. Her values – hard work, high moral standards, civic obligation, and individual responsibility – were values widely shared within the dominant culture of Victorian social reform. Both her parents and she herself believed in ameliorist, evolutionary and parliamentary reform. They were Liberals, not revolutionary socialists, who shared a deep commitment to racial and female equality and to working-class emancipation. She was clearly radicalised, like so many of her generation, by the political atmosphere of mid-Victorian reform politics, and the early years of her life reveal her attachment to contemporary patterns of thinking and behaviour which help explain the choices that she was to make as an adult. For all the excitement about her modernising approach to twentieth-century social policy, we should remember that her belief system never really wavered – it remained firmly grounded in the same nineteenth century radical-Liberalism that she had first encountered as a child.

2

THE LIBERAL YEARS 1880–94

Emmeline Pankhurst, now aged 22 and safely married, could, like so many women of her class, have concentrated on being a wife, house-keeper, and future mother. Theoretically she enjoyed few individual, economic or social rights, but she was never tempted to inhabit what has been termed the 'gilded cage' of bourgeois marriage. Indeed, the Pankhursts reconfigured the social conventions around marriage to suit their political beliefs, regarding it as axiomatic that their partnership was to be a true union of equals, a companionate marriage rather than one in which the wife was subordinate to her husband. Her marriage enabled Emmeline to put into practice the liberal ideas which had been coming into ever sharper focus throughout her childhood, adolescence and early womanhood. Her family background had not only shaped her character; it had given her an idealistic and radical outlook on life. The marriage to Richard Pankhurst consolidated this, and she created a style of living with him which was largely unimpressed by conventional atti-tudes and expectations.

As a young married woman in her twenties, Emmeline was to learn the tools of her political trade. It was in this period of her life that she transformed many of the ideals and principles she had taken for granted as a child into hard political agendas: her commitment to democracy, to women's suffrage and to the poor. In addition, her interest in prostitu-tion, which evolved into a campaign against the white slave trade, had its origins during this period. Her character too was maturing, and she was beginning to exhibit some of the character traits which later came to be recognised as her own distinctive style. We can detect, even at this early stage of her career, something of her formidable energy, her insistent, almost obsessive nature and her love of hard work. Here too we can identify her distaste for compromise and ability to act firmly and decisively. Above all, we encounter the first public manifestations of her deep-seated idealism and her commitment to the notion of justice – at whatever cost to her personal life.

WIFE AND MOTHER

For the first few years of her marriage Emmeline conformed to a more or less conventional Victorian domestic ideal: she stayed at home, devoted her energies to her new family, and had little time left to engage in political activity. In nine years, between 1880 and 1889, she gave birth to five children and witnessed the death of a young son. Her eldest, Christabel, was born on September 22nd 1880, just over nine months after her marriage. Sylvia was born in 1882, Francis Henry (Frank) in 1884, Adela in 1885 and her last child, Henry Francis (Harry), in 1889. In 1885, after living a rather nomadic existence in Manchester, the family moved to Hampstead, London. In 1889 her son Francis Henry (Frank) became ill while she was visiting her husband in Manchester. Soon after she returned Frank died of diphtheria brought on, according to Sylvia, by the defective drains in the house in which they lived. Following Frank's death, the Pankhursts moved from Hampstead to Russell Square. Henry Francis (Harry) was born ten months after Francis Henry (Frank) died. The psychological implications of giving a son his dead brother's name are clear. As Sylvia noted, 'to my mother the expected infant was "Frank coming again" '.[1]

All of the children, save Christabel, suffered from benign neglect and all experienced an erratic and sometimes unorthodox education. As with most children of their class, they were left in the charge of servants for most of their young lives. Sylvia remembers being very severely treated – on one occasion she was tied to a bed for the day for refusing to take cod liver oil – and goes on to comment that her mother was a strict disciplinarian who believed that children should be obedient and respectful to adults. None of the children went to school until they left Russell Square in the winter of 1892–3 to return to the north. Until that time, they were educated – somewhat unsystematically – by either governesses or their aunt, Mary. The children were given access to a wide range of books on philosophy, history and science and spent most of their days reading and drawing. By the age of 10 Sylvia had read Dickens, Edward Lear, William Morris, George Eliot and Charles Kingsley. When an artist friend was employed as governess, the children regularly visited the British Museum to look at the Egyptian collections. In 1893 Emmeline Pankhurst and her children moved to an apartment in the seaside town of Southport and the children eventually went, on Richard Pankhurst's insistence, to a state school. Christabel, now aged 12, and Sylvia, now aged 10, were enrolled in Southport Proprietary School, a High School for Girls, but they only stayed at the school for one term because the family moved to Disley, a village a short distance from Manchester. Here they helped with the harvest, picked blackberries and journeyed out into the countryside in a pony and trap when the weather permitted. Later that year the family returned to Daisy Bank Road, Manchester, where, now recovering from the death of one son and the birth of another, Emmeline apparently recovered her zest for politics. All three girls later attended Manchester High School, whereas Harry was sent to a school managed by an elderly gentleman. Later Sylvia enrolled at Manchester Art School and Christabel went to Switzerland to stay with Noémie Rocheforte, her mother's oldest friend.

Education, according to Emmeline Pankhurst, should extend far beyond the boundaries of school or college. Part of the children's education of course was in politics. Both Christabel and Sylvia joined the Clarion Cyclists' Club, distributing socialist leaflets throughout northern villages and singing socialist songs. The family were regular visitors to the Clarion Cyclists' Camp. Waxing rather lyrically on the benefits of the open air, Emmeline Pankhurst proclaimed that she was 'most glad to come to this Camp with our children, to enter heartily into this common life of recreation and enjoyment. It was a happy stroke of wise choice to pitch your tents by the country side, amid the green and freshness of nature.'[2] Occasionally the children would visit the homes of other political activists. Harriot Stanton Blatch, now living in Basingstoke, invited Christabel and Sylvia to stay with her to keep her daughter, Nora, company. It is evident that the Pankhurst children were brought up in a radical political atmosphere, their behaviour conditioned by a framework of rights and responsibilities. It is almost as if

Emmeline Pankhurst's management of her household prefigured the way she would later run her political campaigns.

WORK

Richard Pankhurst, although a barrister, rarely made much money from his practice so the family were in constant financial difficulties. When the Pankhurst family moved to London, Emmeline opened a fancy goods shop in order to avoid further financial embarrassment. It was named *Emmerson's*, probably after the famous American revolutionary, and there she sold up-market household goods many of which she and her sister painted by hand. Unfortunately, the shop was situated in a rather insalubrious part of Hampstead Road and it proved desperately unsuccessful. Rather than admit failure, however, the shop was re-opened first in Berners Street and later in Regent Street. Her new home in Russell Square, the site today of the Hotel Russell, was sumptuously decorated with the remains of the Hampstead shop. It was lit in the evenings with oil lamps rather than gas in order to create an exotic, romantic atmosphere. Sylvia recollected that 'Chinese tea-pots, old Persian plates, Japanese embroidery, Indian brasses, rugs from Turkey, silks from Wardle's of Leek, cretonnes by Morris and his imitators' were all brought to their new home in Russell Square. Apparently, her mother 'revelled in the gorgeous colours of the Orient and all that was brilliant and bizarre in old art and new.'[3] Unfortunately, the two shops went the same way as the Hampstead Road enterprise – neither of them was profitable but Emmeline's perseverance would always override failure.

The Pankhurst homes, just like her parents', were always full of visiting political activists. The first sitting-room of their house in Russell Square, London, was a centre of meetings and conferences: for women's rights, the Abolition of the House of Lords, Radicalism, Republicanism, Agnosticism, Socialism, the New Trade Unionism. Guests at Russell Square included Jacob Bright, Dadabhai Neroji (the first Indian to become an MP), Henry Rochefort, Louise Michel (heroine of the Paris Commune), Annie Besant, Elizabeth Cady Stanton, her daughter Harriot Stanton Blatch and William Lloyd Garrison (leader of the American anti-slavery movement). Mr Mulvi, a servant of Queen Victoria who was teaching Her Majesty Hindustani, was also a frequent visitor. Similarly, in Manchester the Pankhursts' various houses were a 'home from home of Socialist agitators'. Keir Hardie, Bruce and Katherine Glasier, Fred Brocklehurst, Ramsay MacDonald and his future wife Margaret Gladstone, and the German revolutionaries Karl W. Liebknecht and Eleanor Marx all visited.[4]

ELECTION CAMPAIGNS

Women of all political persuasions shared the common goal of electing men who shared their political perspective, often organising entire electoral campaigns for their male relatives. Emmeline Pankhurst worked hard to promote her husband in three elections: in 1883 as an Independent, in 1885 as a Radical-Liberal and in 1895 as an ILP candidate. He lost all three.

The first time Richard Pankhurst stood for Parliament was as an Independent candidate in an 1883 Manchester by-election. The executive of the Manchester Liberal Association and the two Liberal newspapers in the country refused to support him and instructed electors not to vote for 'the Doctor'.[5] Without formal political party support and the party machinery to organise the election campaign, Richard's parliamentary career was likely to flounder. Although his catchy 'Government of the Nation, by the Nation, for the Nation' slogan was an inspired one, his extreme radical and idealistic programme did not help. He advocated free secular education; the disestablishment of the Church and the secularisation of all political institutions; the abolition of the monarchy and the House of Lords; full adult suffrage; the payment of MPs; nationalisation of the land; and, probably most unpopular of all, Home Rule for Ireland.

Without Liberal Party support Richard relied on his family to help. Despite having two young children, Christabel and Sylvia, both under the age of 3, Emmeline worked tirelessly to help her husband get elected. Her father, Robert Goulden, represented Richard as his election agent in the constituency, and took responsibility for organising the election campaign. But despite all this family assistance, Richard was doomed to fail. He was 'considerably disliked by a large section of the Liberals, whose nerves he is apt to startle in a very reckless fashion'.[6] In addition, probably because of lack of money as much as moral principle, he abided by the principles of the new Corrupt Practices Act which was about to come into force, whereas his opponent did not. The Corrupt

Practices Act, 1883, limited the number of paid canvassers who could be employed and forbade treating, bribing or hiring of vehicles to take electors to the polls. Consequently, Richard Pankhurst's electoral expenses were £500, whereas his opponent's reached a staggering £5,000.[7] Not surprisingly, given all the constraints, he only polled 6,216 votes, whereas the Conservative candidate won 18,188.

Not only did he lose the election, he forfeited the support of his father-in-law. Robert Goulden made clear his displeasure at his son-in-law's increasingly radical politics – his business had suffered as a result of Richard's electoral programme and he refused to jeopardise his financial security any further. After the 1883 by-election a pregnant Emmeline, Richard, their two small girls and Emmeline's sister Mary left the Goulden family home in Seedley, where they had been living. Emmeline, who had once been close to her father, now severed all contact with him. They were never to see each other again. In 1892 her father, by now aged 60, died of apoplexy while visiting his holiday cottage on the Isle of Man. His funeral, which took place on April 24th, was attended by all but one of his surviving children. Emmeline, estranged from her father for almost ten years, was absent. Throughout her life, she was to place politics above people; she was never afraid to break with those dear to her if they disagreed with her own fundamental values or beliefs. Of course, she had clashed with her father before, in particular over her prospective marriage to a Frenchman, so family conflict was not new.

Two years later, in 1885, Richard Pankhurst stood as Liberal and Radical candidate for Rotherhithe, London, in the general election of that year. In her autobiography it was called 'a riverside constituency', whereas in reality it was a poor working-class district in the heart of the docklands. Emmeline Pankhurst 'threw herself heart and soul' into the campaign, much to the astonishment of the local population, who were unaccustomed to the sight of a woman campaigning so energetically.[8] Persistence was seen to be one of her leading qualities early in her political career. On one occasion she wrote to the leading suffragist Caroline Biggs to ask if anything could be done by 'our suffrage friends' to assist in her husband's election. 'Will the women of London assist him in his Candidature? Dr Pankhurst's long connection with and the services he has rendered to the cause of Women's Suffrage justly entitle him to any aid they may give in the contest which no doubt will be a severe one.'[9]

After a vigorous campaign, and despite official support from the Liberals, Richard once again lost to the Conservative candidate. Emmeline blamed his defeat on Irish Home Rulers – this can be seen as the beginning of her volatile relationship with Irish politics. In this election the Irish electorate were advised by the Irish leader, Charles Stewart Parnell, to vote against any Liberal candidate (even if he supported Home Rule) and for the Tories. The principled Richard Pankhurst supported Home Rule and so lost the votes of those who wanted to keep Ireland united with Britain. Yet he did not gain the support of the Catholic vote because of Parnell's instructions. Although the precise impact of the Irish vote outside Ireland is a matter of historical conjecture, Emmeline saw Parnell's tactical political manoeuvrings as the decisive factor in her husband's defeat. Such methods, she said, were a 'valuable political lesson, one that years later I was destined to put into practice'.[10]

Emmeline Pankhurst's analysis of her husband's defeat was somewhat flawed. In many ways Richard was as much the victim of Liberal Party national politics and internal conflict as of Irish agitation. By the mid-1880s the Liberal Party was rent with divisions: over Home Rule for Ireland; over Free Trade versus Protection; over land, educational and local government reform; over principles of taxation; and over imperialist policies. It was also becoming increasingly unpopular. There was a strong anti-Liberal vote in the cities: apart from Birmingham, which remained solidly Liberal, the Conservatives won 116 out of 226 borough constituencies. The final electoral result led to deadlock, with the Irish Party under Parnell holding the political balance in the House of Commons: Conservatives 249; Liberals 335 and the Irish under Parnell 86. The balance of power in the House of Commons now lay with the Irish Party, a situation that again proved to be a formative influence on the developing political consciousness of Emmeline Pankhurst.

The unelectability of Liberals in general, combined with Richard Pankhurst's radical politics, meant that his chances of election were as remote as ever. Again, his political programme was extremely left-wing. He insisted that the hereditary element of the House of Lords be abolished 'at once and absolutely', arguing that as there should be 'no privileged power in class, so we must have no privileged institutions in society'. He also advocated the disestablishment of the Church of England, free education and 'the distribution of wealth'.[11] And he continued to support Home Rule. Helen Taylor, the unconventional step-daughter of John Stuart Mill, who campaigned for him wearing trousers, may also have shocked and alienated the local electorate.

Moreover, during the election campaign there was a lot of mud-slinging by the Conservative candidate, who publicly accused Richard Pankhurst of atheism. Both the Pankhursts were physically assaulted: he was pelted with stones, she with muck and refuse from the market. For Emmeline it was a savage introduction to politics. After the election the Pankhursts brought a libel action against the Conservative MP as a test case 'which would show how far socialist candidates could find remedy in the new libel law for the flood of slanderous abuse that was turned on them at every election'.[12] When Richard lost the libel case, Emmeline accused the judge of 'lending his aid to a disreputable section of the Tory Party' and of supporting the Conservatives at the expense of justice.[13] As the wife of a leading lawyer, she must have been all too aware of the legal implications of her statement – she could have been put on trial for contempt of court and fined or imprisoned. Her determination to seek justice at whatever the personal cost was, and would continue to be, a characteristic of her personality. Fortunately, the judge ignored her letter and the incident faded away in the public memory. Eventually Richard Pankhurst, who took the case to the Court of Queen's Bench, was awarded damages fixed at £60, a small and derisory sum, but one which both of them were quick to claim as a moral victory.

WOMEN'S RIGHTS AND WOMEN'S SUFFRAGE

From an early age, Emmeline Pankhurst was a true democrat who believed in Parliament and the parliamentary process. An evolutionary rather than a revolutionary socialist, she was committed to radical change through constitutional means, not through violent upheaval. Wanting women to be part of the political world, she joined – and founded – a number of suffrage organisations with the aim of achieving this worthy ambition. Yet, although in later life she was to blaze a glorious trail on behalf of women's suffrage, her work in the early suffrage movement was initially insignificant and for much of the time she remained on the sidelines of women's politics. Nevertheless, these early experiences in the emerging women's suffrage movement would undoubtedly shape the way in which she would plan, organise and enact her campaigns in the future.

The late nineteenth-century women's suffrage movement, in common with most radical organisations, was characterised by internal factions. Like other political associations with just one goal, and often without any real power, the suffragists and later the suffragettes differed over the best way to achieve their objective. In 1879, just a few months before she married, Emmeline joined a recently united organisation, the National Society for Women's Suffrage (NSWS), under the leadership of Lydia Becker. Soon she was voted on to the executive of the NSWS – some say in honour of Richard Pankhurst, who had worked with Lydia Becker for some years, rather than on her own merit. However, she was largely inactive for the first few years because of new family responsibilities. In 1883, when Christabel and Sylvia were infants and just before the last three of her children were born, she began to take a more prominent role,[14] and was very active in the NSWS campaign to include a women's suffrage amendment to the 1884 County Franchise Bill. Unfortunately, Gladstone, the Liberal Prime Minister, refused to accept the Bill and ordered Liberal MPs to vote against it, so it failed.

Throughout her entire life, Emmeline Pankhurst was unyielding in her political convictions and, consequently, her whole suffrage career was marked by feuding and discord. Although a political activist, she was never gifted with the negotiating skills of other suffrage leaders such as Millicent Fawcett, who was willing to do deals, compromise and seek the middle ground. Throughout her life Emmeline rarely refused to bend her fiercely held convictions, preferring full-frontal attacks to circuitous and cautious discussion. Overall, generally fuelled by disagreements, she belonged to at least five different women's suffrage organisations: the newly united National Society for Women's Suffrage (NSWS), the National Central Society for Women's Suffrage, the Women's Franchise League, the National Union of Women's Suffrage Societies and her own – soon to be notorious – Women's Social and Political Union.

At the end of 1888 she was embroiled in the first of her many major disagreements over political strategy. This occurred when she, along with a number of mostly younger and radical suffragists, wanted the NSWS to affiliate to the women's section of the Liberal Association. At the time, both Pankhursts were staunch Radical-Liberals, and to link women's suffrage to a party which was perceived to be sympathetic to votes for women was thought to be fruitful for both sides. Others – mostly older members like Lydia Becker – disagreed because they wanted to keep women's suffrage independent of party politics. It certainly seemed as if her loyalty to party overrode her allegiance to women's suffrage, but she may have genuinely believed that the Liberal Party was fully committed to votes for women. In addition, she wanted to link suffrage with other female reforms (in particular the campaign for greater property rights), while the older members preferred to keep suffrage distinct. As a consequence, the suffrage movement split into two groups: the National Central Society for Women's Suffrage (known as Great College St), which Emmeline Pankhurst joined; and Lydia Becker's Central Committee of the National Society for Women's Suffrage (known as Parliament St). Lydia Becker, who had devoted her entire life to the suffrage movement, regarded the Pankhurst wing as left-wing and extreme.

WOMEN'S FRANCHISE LEAGUE

Soon Emmeline Pankhurst was disagreeing with the policies of the newly formed National Central Society (NCS). The NCS wanted to restrict the vote to single women, which meant that married women would be excluded from the franchise. Both Pankhursts criticised this policy – and the Society – for its willingness to sacrifice married women to achieve a limited goal.[15] In their view, the exclusion of married women from the vote was unjustifiable. 'I think,' Richard argued, 'it would push back freedom for married women certainly twenty or five-and-twenty years.'[16] The question of which women should be given the vote was a matter of deep contention within the suffrage movement. Some suffragists insisted that it was better to have a small reform rather than no reform at all. Emmeline had no sympathy whatever for this view and so, on July 25th 1889, just after the birth of her first son, she helped to establish the Women's Franchise League (WFrL).[17] From the very beginning, this new organisation, like the NCS from which she resigned, identified with the Liberal Party. At the time Emmeline and Richard were Radical-Liberals, and the Liberal MP Jacob Bright, who was one of the chief spokesmen for women's suffrage in Parliament, was another founding member. Their new organisation had two main aims, firstly 'to extend to women, whether unmarried, married or widowed, the right to vote at Parliamentary, Municipal, Local and other elections'[18] on the same terms as men, and secondly to 'establish for all women equal civil and political rights with men'.[19] It was the first women's suffrage society to include married women in the franchise.

Emmeline Pankhurst was elected on to the Provisional Executive Committee of the WFrL alongside three other women and three men. However, often men did the speaking at the meetings while women sat and listened. She did not speak at the inaugural meeting but her husband spoke at inordinate length – much longer than any other speaker did – on the history of women's suffrage, a story that must have been well known to everyone present. Lloyd Garrison and Harriot Stanton Blatch also contributed but very briefly – presumably because Richard had taken up most of the allotted time.[20] According to Sylvia Pankhurst, her mother became very involved in Franchise League functions, 'arranging elaborate teas, music by celebrated artists, speeches by famous people'.[21] Nevertheless, there is evidence that she also helped frame organisational policy. In 1894 she put forward a resolution to Parliament condemning the Cambridge Corporation for upholding a double standard of sexual morality and eroding the personal rights of the working class. She accused them of giving police too much power to arrest and 'imprison any woman whom they may suspect of being an immoral person, even if she be quietly walking in the street and molesting no one'.[22]

The WFrL was a small organisation with many influential members. The Council included many of the radical luminaries of the period: Jacob Bright, Josephine Butler, Elizabeth Wolstenholme-Elmy, William Lloyd Garrison and Harriot Stanton Blatch. The WFrL was certainly successful in attracting top Liberal support. In November 1889 it hosted a well-attended meeting at which R.B. Haldane was a keynote speaker. In the near future Haldane was to introduce a Women's Electoral Franchise Bill prepared by the WFrL, which enabled every woman who possessed the rate-paying or other legal qualifications to vote on the same terms as men 'without status as maiden, wife or widow.'[23] Haldane's Bill failed. Again, Emmeline claimed in her autobiography that 'it was never taken seriously by the Government',[24] although she was optimistic at the time about the chances of success.

In December 1891 the Women's Franchise League appeared to be robust. As *The Graphic*, a paper not known for its commitment to suffrage, reported: 'Last week witnessed an unusual wave of activity upon the subject of the enfranchisement of women, and meetings and debates took place at several centres. This gathering was held at the house of Dr and Mrs Pankhurst, 8 Russell Square, and the "Conference", as it was called, lasted for three evenings.'[25] The leading Radical-Liberals James Stansfeld, R.B. Haldane and Jacob Bright were present to lend support. A different topic was discussed each evening. The first session (chaired by James Stansfeld) focused on the education, training, occupation, rates of pay, hours and working conditions of female workers; the second concentrated on political rights and duties and the parliamentary and local franchise; the third (chaired by Richard Pankhurst) looked at the programme of the WFrL and its activities.[26] Attempts were made by the WFrL to bridge the suffrage gap and to re-unite the suffrage movement but the other societies were reluctant to join. A leading member of the NSWS, Mrs Eva McLaren, 'said that as Dr. Pankhurst showed signs of his intention to boss the whole business, they [i.e. the NSWS] had backed out and declined further union'.[27]

Even the unity of this small group was not to last and a year later a third split occurred. Many historians date Emmeline Pankhurst's suffrage militancy from 1905, but she was involved in disruptive behaviour long before this time. In April 1892 the Pankhursts caused a disturbance at a suffrage meeting organised by Lydia Becker in St James' Hall, because they disagreed with her suffrage policies. At the time a Parliamentary Franchise Bill, put forward as a private member's bill by the Conservative MP Albert Rollitt, was being discussed in Parliament. Lydia Becker, who called the meeting in support of Rollitt, championed this Bill, which would enfranchise single, but not married, women. Both Pankhursts heckled the speakers; they interrupted proceedings by shouting their objections to this limited franchise and demanding that married women be included. The upshot of the Pankhursts' behaviour was to produce further splits within the suffrage movement. Elizabeth Wolstenholme-Elmy, critical of their disorderly behaviour, resigned from her position as Secretary of the Women's Franchise League. Instead of trying to placate her friend and erstwhile ally, Emmeline supported Ursula Bright's appointment as Secretary and became an honorary secretary herself. With Ursula Bright's appointment, the links between the WFrL and the Liberal Party were reaffirmed and consolidated, since the wife of a very senior Liberal MP now headed the organisation.

The promotion of Ursula Bright to the post of Secretary strengthened their friendship. The two activists worked together for the suffrage cause for a number of years, wrote to each other frequently and stayed at each other's homes. Like Emmeline, Ursula Bright was engaged in promoting women in local and national politics. All the hard work put in by these two women and others finally bore fruit in the 1894 Local Government Act. This Act enshrined the principle that all women, whether married or single, should be entitled to vote in local elections if they possessed the necessary property qualifications. Ursula Bright's husband, Jacob, was primarily responsible for securing this municipal franchise, while Richard Pankhurst had drafted the Bill. Not surprisingly, Emmeline and Ursula were delighted. In a triumphalist letter to her friend, Ursula commented that the other two, rival, societies 'are simply mad at our success. They never calculated upon such a decisive victory ... it will be impossible to carry a Parliamentary spinster's Bill if the married women are locally enfranchised.'[28] In fact, the assertion that it would now be impossible to exclude married women from the franchise was in some ways prophetic; the 1894 Local Government Act had the effect of collapsing many of the old animosities between different suffrage societies. With married women safely enfranchised in local government, it seemed nonsensical, and possibly even churlish, to insist that only single women be given the vote. By the end of the nineteenth century, all suffrage societies were committed to campaigning for women to be given the vote on the same terms as men.

It is important to remember that the continuous bickering and disagreements within the suffrage movement were good for the refinement of ideas and policy. Indeed, the splits and divisions which occurred within the societies can be seen to have had a positively creative and generative function – their dynamics were instrumental in shaping new organisational directions for the twentieth century.[29] More importantly for Emmeline Pankhurst's own political career, she learned a very great deal about organisational strategy even though the WFrL itself was very short-lived. As Harriot Stanton Blatch later wrote of the WFrL, 'there rose from its ashes the militant work of the WSPU in England and the work of the Women's Political Union in America.'[30]

CONCLUSION

In 1892 the Pankhursts returned to live in Manchester, becoming increasingly disillusioned with the Liberal leadership. In 1894 they resigned from the Liberal Party to join the Independent Labour Party (ILP). This was not because they were drifting even further leftwards – the break was about the performance of the Liberal Party in office rather than about underlying principles. The Pankhursts broke with the Liberal Party at the very moment it became apparent that it was unable to deliver its radical programme. In the early 1880s the Liberal Party was in the mainstream of progressive politics, and those concerned with social questions joined or voted for it. This supremacy was not to last. In 1886 the Liberal Party split over the question of Home Rule and remained weak and divided on the matter for some time. Moreover, in 1894, when Gladstone resigned from his fourth and last ministry, the party lacked leadership. The next leader, the patrician and aristocratic Earl of Rosebery, would not have appealed to the Pankhursts' democratic inclinations. The divisions within and the near-destruction of the Liberal Party coincided with the establishment of the Independent Labour Party. It was in the context of this Liberal diaspora, rather than over policy differences, that they both left to join the newly emerging ILP.

The Pankhursts did not shift their political principles but merely, as with many others, abandoned the Liberal Party as the instrument with which to gain them. The early ILP was said to be a 'synthesis of many different strands of socialist thinking' with no clearly defined ideology apart from aiming to obtain mass support of the working class and to take the parliamentary, as opposed to the revolutionary, road to socialism.[31] The ILP would have appealed to the Pankhursts because it would have reminded them of the old-style Liberal radicalism that was by now terminally weakened if not altogether defunct. Certainly some of its early policies were suggestive of Chamberlain's 'Unauthorised Programme', in which he advocated land reform, free education, local government reform, progressive taxation and disestablishment of the Church and spoke tantalisingly of the 'rights of property'. The ILP usurped and developed this radical programme by calling for the collective ownership of the means of production, distribution and exchange, advocating an eight-hour day, a minimum wage, powers for local bodies to acquire land and capital to ensure employment, state pensions and free education to university level.

According to Christabel Pankhurst, her mother was keener to join the ILP than her father, who feared social ostracism and further decline in his financial fortunes. Emmeline was attracted to the ILP because it declared itself sympathetic to the emancipation of women; it claimed that women were equal to men within the party and encouraged women to play a central role in formulating policy.[32] It certainly considered itself the first political party to give unconditional support to the women's suffrage cause. However, its support was relatively lukewarm, for although some members supported female suffrage wholeheartedly, others viewed women's rights as a middle-class individualistic movement that embodied a liberal, rather than a socialist, philosophy. For many ILP members there was no commitment to prioritise women's struggle at the expense of workers' rights.

A number of defining principles were beginning to take shape at this time. Emmeline's awareness of Irish strategic policy, her use of disruptive tactics to gain a political end, her increasing commitment to full democracy, her belief in some elements of nationalisation and her dedication to the alleviation of poverty were all in evidence at this time. She also demonstrated some temperamental characteristics: an emotional response to politics; a commitment to fight against social and political injustices; an inability to compromise deeply felt principles; a willingness to offend and to fight her corner. These, as well as her idiosyncratic individualism, were evident as traits which would continue to be enduring marks of her political personality. Indeed her beliefs changed less than the politics of the parties she supported. Her radical political inclinations emerged very early on and some of her principles remained fairly constant: her parliamentarianism, her republicanism, her support for women's franchise, her commitment to equal opportunities for women, her ideas for helping to alleviate or end poverty and her beliefs about social purity.

3

THE ILP YEARS 1894–1903

In May 1896 Emmeline Pankhurst, encouraged by her husband, tore down fences in a public park near Manchester in protest at the curbing of free speech. It was her first public outburst of violence. The local authority, which had previously banned the Independent Labour Party (ILP) from speaking there, had erected fences to stop audiences from congregating in the area. Undeterred, ILP members continued to speak in the park and so were charged, summonsed, put on trial, and imprisoned. Eventually, after a lot of news coverage and various legal battles, the ILP won. This dramatic episode encouraged Emmeline to believe that when respectable middle-class people broke the law, it generated publicity and led to victory.

The nine years between 1894 and 1903 represent the period of Emmeline's most active political commitment to her new organisation, the Independent Labour Party (ILP). Most of the time she was engaged in peaceful, rather than militant action, acting as an ILP representative of the Poor Law Guardians and on Education Committees. In January 1895 she was elected Vice-President of the Manchester and Salford District ILP and a few years later, at the Sixth Annual Conference in April 1898, she was elected to the ILP Executive, the National Administrative Council (NAC). Here she joined an illustrious group that included Keir Hardie, John Bruce Glasier, Ramsay MacDonald and Philip Snowden. She was not the first woman to be elected on to the

NAC – two others had served in previous years – but she was the only woman that year. Altogether she secured 77 votes, two votes more than a future prime minister, Ramsay MacDonald, and 39 more than a future chancellor of the exchequer, Philip Snowden. She was also elected on to the Publishing Committee responsible for the production and issue of the newly created *ILP News*.[1] At the same conference in 1898 she was elected to be the official organiser and co-ordinator of ILP Poor Law Guardians. In 1902 she proposed a motion on women's suffrage at the Annual Conference which was adopted. She remained an active and influential member of the ILP until her commitment to women's suffrage clashed with party policies and, after much protracted discussion, she eventually left.

This period marks a significant advance in her political maturation. Emmeline Pankhurst was similar to other socialist women who, as June Hannam and Karen Hunt observe, were 'flouting convention in two ways, by taking part in public actions which could be viewed as "unwomanly" and by supporting a "subversive" doctrine'.[2] In Emmeline's early married life, she inevitably took a supporting role to help promote Richard's political career but now her own political identity begins to emerge. This is perhaps most clearly seen in her involvement in local politics; her work as Poor Law Guardian and on Manchester School Board helped shape the political road map she was to follow throughout her life. These early years were not marginal areas of her life, since it was through the prism of poverty and education that she began to formulate her own principles, an agenda which was always staunchly pro-woman. In a letter to Emma Sproson, a radical suffragist and socialist, she wrote: 'I am arranging to speak only where [ILP] Branches desire me to deal mainly with the woman side of socialism. There are plenty of speakers on the general question and the woman's side has until lately been neglected.'[3] Here, and in her other political commitments, her involvement in a cause or issue was underpinned by strong feelings, often expressed in passionate outbursts. She may have changed political parties but she continued to fight for her cherished principles with the idealism of a fundamentalist. Her adherence to politics may have been doctrinal at times but her commitment was generally to 'big ideas' rather than formal political parties. Emmeline's style gave very little room for negotiation: she would assess others' opinions as starkly right or wrong and was, as usual, seemingly unaffected by the tensions she generated with colleagues by taking either extreme or unpopular political positions.

POOR LAW GUARDIAN

The Independent Labour Party (ILP) urged its members to become involved in local politics so that they could help alleviate poverty. In particular, ILP activists were encouraged to stand for Poor Law elections so that they could improve the lives of workhouse inmates. Emmeline, agreeing with this tactic, argued that 'by manning and *woman*ing' the Boards of Guardians changes would be made which would improve the lives of the working class in their locality.[4] There may have been other reasons, apart from a wish to improve the well-being of the working class, behind her decision to stand as a Poor Law Guardian. After women had obtained the vote, she advised a 17-year-old young woman (who later became an MP) to 'start with Local Government. The work will give you insight and knowledge at first hand of people and their needs, and a complete understanding of parish and borough council administration will help you later on to understand the Parliamentary system.'[5] Indeed, even though women did not have the vote, local government work was seen to be a good apprenticeship for future parliamentary politics, since it gave women valuable political training in canvassing, leafleting, petitioning, organising elections, public speaking and dealing with hecklers. It also trained women in committee work, which often meant putting forward unpopular policies to predominantly male committees. Moreover, by engaging in useful public duties, such as Poor Law work, women would prove that they were fit and ready for the vote. Emmeline wrote later of her work in the Poor Law: 'We did it in the hope that we should convince them and persuade them to do the right and proper thing'[6] – that is enfranchise women.

In 1894 Emmeline Pankhurst was elected as Poor Law Guardian for Openshaw as an ILP representative. She was elected unopposed, and at the head of the polls, on the two occasions she sought election.[7] Of course, this might have had less to do with her popularity than with the reluctance of women to take part, for, despite pleas from herself and from the ILP leadership, few women were willing to stand as Poor Law Guardians because the work was so unpleasant. All too often women dealt with the most distressed social groups, for 'into the workhouse came the sick whom voluntary hospitals would not nurse; the diseased and mentally disturbed, the brazen and the depraved; the derelicts, the drunks, and the tramps'.[8] It took an uncommon sort of woman to get involved in Poor Law work since it required considerable courage, compassion and obduracy: Emmeline had a good supply of all.

Attitudes towards the Poor Law

It seems surprising that, given her radical inclinations, she was content to work within the limitations of the Poor Law legislation. She never mounted, in public at least, devastating attacks of the sort made by the socialist MP George Lansbury and others on the failures of the workhouse system.[9] George Lansbury, who was elected Poor Law Guardian for Poplar, East London, in 1892, was scathing about the way in which workhouse inmates were degraded. He eventually persuaded the Poplar Guardians to adopt a policy of giving generous outdoor relief to those in need: a system which became known – and either praised or derided – as 'Poplarism'. In fact, very few of the new women Guardians criticised the principles of the 1834 Act. Most, like Emmeline, tried to implement the existing provisions fairly and equitably and tried to work within the system rather than undermine or challenge it. Indeed, she insisted that it was the administrators, rather than the Poor Law itself, who were responsible for the Guardians' negative image. 'The men elected on the Boards of Guardians,' she claimed, 'frequently lose sight of the fact that they are Guardians of the Poor and make themselves the Guardians of the Rates.'[10] She believed that the Poor Law had considerable power whose 'exercise is virtually stopped by a network of regulations that neutralises the law.'[11] Poor Law authorities, she asserted, were crippled by a centralised administrative system that undermined attempts at social justice. 'When I came into office,' she insisted, 'I found that the law in our district, Chorlton, was being very harshly administered.' She wanted to improve the Poor Law system not to abolish it.

Poor Law work, despite its negative image, was often seen to be suitable for women because it was viewed as 'public housekeeping'. Caring for children and old people, nursing the sick, supervising food and running a home were thought to be women's work not men's.[12] Workhouses, it was argued, 'require for their management the home knowledge and domestic experience which is the special sphere of women'.[13] Certainly, Emmeline's household management skills were put to use in the workhouse. She focused her main energies on improving conditions; her daughter Sylvia stated that her mother 'was resourceful in securing the alleviation of their drab lot .... A touch of home, a glint of the motherly house-wife's common-sense, she imported into the workhouse.'[14] For the most part, obviously still at ease with old-style Liberal categorisations rather than radical-socialist, she concentrated on improving the conditions of those she saw as the 'deserving' poor: children, women, the elderly and those who were unemployed through no fault of their own.

Helping children

Emmeline Pankhurst believed that children should not be placed in workhouses. In the workhouse she was 'horrified' to see 7 and 8-year-old girls, dressed in thin cotton frocks, scrubbing the stone floors. She was equally shocked that these same girls wore nothing at all at night because nightdresses were considered too good for pauper children. She insisted that the 'little girls' should have nightdresses and knickers, which they lacked when she first came – 'little things but received with great gratitude in those days'.[15] In the longer term, she advocated a similar system to that practised in Sheffield and West Derby, whereby workhouse children were sent to live under the care of matrons in houses dispersed throughout the city. These children attended their local Board school, mixed with other non-pauper children and wore ordinary clothes rather than workhouse uniform. The Guardians aimed 'to rear them in the nearest approach to home life ... without the fear of the taint of pauperism clinging to them'.

Never one for abstract politics, she used her position on the Building Committee of the Chorlton Guardians to encourage the building of cottage homes at Styal for the pauper children in her district. 'Mrs Pankhurst made this her special work, and from the digging of the foundation of the homes she did not miss more than two meetings of the Building Committee, of which she was the only lady member.'[16] The houses, completed a month after she had resigned as Poor Law Guardian in August 1898, were a tribute to her dogged perseverance and diligence. She even persuaded the Guardians to erect a gymnasium, swimming baths and a school for the Styal children.[17] But her work here was not all above criticism; the cottage homes at Styal were built against the wishes of the Gregg family, the Nonconformist and philanthropic owners of Styal mill, who feared it would decrease the value of their land and the property on it. Mr Gregg sent a letter to the Guardians arguing that if the new buildings were to be erected 'his choice sites for first class villa residences would be ruined … he regarded the erection of an establishment for 300 pauper children on the costly residential estate as a death blow to the "privacy, rusticity and out of the worldishness" of the old-fashioned hamlet of Styal, and also to the value of his land.'[18] Mr Gregg's comments were noted by the Guardians and duly ignored.

Emmeline was decidedly unsympathetic to parents who neglected their children. In a speech to the North Western District Poor Law Conference in 1897 she urged that Guardians be given greater powers to protect children with inadequate parents. Britain, she argued, should copy other 'civilised nations' who took away parental rights when a child's welfare was endangered. She recommended adopting French law, whereby drunken, immoral parents who ill-treated their children had them taken away. 'In child protection and child saving,' she argued, 'this country can and ought to lead the way. Our Poor Law in its principle and legal foundation provides a basis on which to ground a legislation of comprehensive and far-reaching order.'[19] Only by utilising the full power of the state, she argued, could children be saved. Her compassion for children was mixed with pragmatism. She promoted this course of action because children of inadequate parents were most likely to become inadequates themselves and thus pose a future threat to the social equilibrium. 'The just and necessary protection of the life and future of the child,' she argued, 'demands that it should have fit conditions for securing 1) health, 2) education, 3) technical teaching and training, 4) moral discipline, 5) a start in life. Deprive the child of these necessary conditions, and how is it to live an honest and useful life! The state of our gaols, workhouses, lunatic asylums, and reformatories gives the answer.'

Caring for the feeble-minded

Emmeline, largely influenced by Mary Dendy, another Poor Law Guardian, became deeply involved with the care and control of children and young people considered to be 'feeble-minded', a quasi-medical term used to classify people who were perceived to be of limited intellectual ability. In 1901, according to statistics from the *Eugenics Review*, there were 818 feeble-minded people in Manchester. Eugenicist theories, that is a belief in the survival of the fittest, determined the perception and treatment of the 'feeble-minded'. It is difficult to gauge her commitment to eugenics but it is safe to say that, like the vast bulk of Victorians, she was not antagonistic to the basic tenets. Indeed, Mary Dendy, with whom Emmeline worked very closely in a number of areas, was a noted eugenicist.

As with other Poor Law Guardians, Emmeline thought that the workhouse, with its meagre diet, its rule-bound regimes and its general atmosphere, was completely unsuitable for those deemed to be 'feeble-minded'. She believed that such individuals needed plenty of fresh air, nutritious food and a certain amount of liberty and diversity in their lives. Unlike many other Guardians, Emmeline never complained about the cost of workhouse provision for the 'feeble-minded' since she believed they were part of the 'deserving' poor. Her primary goal was to bring them under the guardianship of the Board to 'remove from society a grave source of degradation and danger'.[20] By the late nineteenth century it was believed that there were enough 'feeble-minded' in England alone to constitute a separate category of care, and specialist accommodation was created at places such as Earlswood Asylum, Surrey, the Eastern Counties and in some London authorities. Emmeline supported this policy of specialist accommodation and urged other Unions to do whatever they could to combine these 'poor children': 'Think for a moment,' she said, 'of the condition of the respectable working-man who has the misfortune to number in his family a feeble-minded child. Do we [as Guardians] place him in a school where efforts are made to improve his mental condition and some useful occupation taught him, or do we allow him to vegetate?'[21] By the late 1890s she was advocating increased powers of detention for 'feeble-minded' children.

Caring for the elderly

Emmeline was also convinced that the treatment of the *elderly* needed fundamental reform. She may well have been specifically inspired by radicals such as Charles Booth, who in *Life and Labour of the People in*

London revealed that at least one-third of those who reached the age of 70 were forced to accept poor relief, however thrifty they had been when young. In its place he advocated a system of old age pensions. In 1895 a Royal Commission on the Aged Poor criticised the harsh conditions in workhouses and advised that elderly paupers should not be sent to workhouses if they were capable of looking after themselves. Emmeline Pankhurst shared this view and, like Charles Booth, advocated a system of old age pensions. Non-contributory pensions were eventually introduced in 1908 for those over 70 who were of sound moral character and were poor, and in 1911 the National Insurance Act provided health and unemployment insurance for a number of other workers.

At meetings, Emmeline constantly raised the need to improve the care of the elderly. In her own workhouse she found old people 'sitting on backless forms, or benches. They had no privacy, no possessions, not even a locker. The old women were without pockets in their gowns so they were obliged to keep any poor little treasure they had in their bosoms.'[22] She was concerned that married couples lived in unsuitable quarters in 'barrack-like day rooms and dormitories, bare of all comfort'.[23] Female Guardians were slowly raising the standards of comfort for the elderly poor incarcerated in the workhouses and Emmeline Pankhurst was no exception; she reformed her local workhouse, got rid of the workhouse uniform, provided wooden arm chairs, lockers, day rooms and better sleeping facilities and improved the food.[24]

Helping the unemployed

Emmeline believed that society, rather than the individuals concerned, should be blamed for unemployment. Soon after her appointment as Poor Law Guardian in 1894 she was faced with a severe crisis, when a particularly harsh winter led to exceptional distress and widespread poverty in the northern regions. During the winter crisis the workhouse was severely overcrowded – there were no vacant beds on the male side of the house, forcing the Guardians to use the boys' schoolroom as a dormitory.[25]

The Board of Guardians, reluctant to offer outdoor relief, responded to the challenge by offering soup kitchens and appealing to the richer sections of Manchester for charitable help. During this winter crisis 'over seventy voluntary agencies and individuals were giving temporary relief chiefly in the form of soup, bread, clothing and other essential supplies'.[26] Emmeline knew the importance of helping the people she represented and so set about forming, with her husband and other ILP figures, a Committee for the Relief of the Unemployed. She organised street collections, placed advertisements in the press to raise money and set up free canteens for the unemployed and their families. She also 'drove out each morning collecting gifts of food from the stallholders in Shudehill Market and the city merchants, then took her place on a lorry handing out soup and bread.'[27] The ILP men and women cooked the soup in the ILP halls and brought it to Stevenson Square in vans. As a result of these efforts approximately 2,000 people were fed daily in Stevenson Square, Manchester, in Ancoats, in Gorton and in Openshaw.

Charity, however, was not enough, so she urged that the Chorlton Guardians adopt a more pro-active approach. She was highly critical of local government because it 'had absolutely failed in the purpose for which it came into existence ... it had not protected the poor in the smallest degree'.[28] In her view, local government hindered the work of Poor Law Guardians because it prevented them from granting immediate and adequate relief. She wanted a significant policy change, advocated a more centralised strategy and urged Parliament to set up a special committee which would have 'the special and exclusive task of giving full effect to the principles of the Poor Law in their true extent and intention'.[29] Elected representatives, she maintained, should not be governed by a 'bureau composed of paid permanent officials'.[30] At a meeting of the Chorlton Guardians she argued that, as large numbers of people were about to become unemployed, 'it was the duty of the Guardians and other public bodies at once to apply for larger powers to deal with the relief of distress'.[31] Every other member present, apart from one other socialist, disagreed with her.

Poor Law authorities, Emmeline maintained, had a duty to find work for the unemployed and to look after the sick and infirm. For her, the issues were clear. Every man, woman and child had 'the right to live, by work in the case of those who are able to work, without work in the case of the infirm and sick'. She criticised the fact that unemployed people were set to work at stone-breaking or oakum-picking (unpicking ropes) – 'as useless as it is degrading'.[32] In its place, the unemployed should be offered work that maintained their human dignity. She suggested three types of employment for those out of work and too poor to keep themselves: '1) employment on the land in various modes of work, 2) employment on public works in new constructions, as well as in extensions, improvements and repair of those now existing, 3) employment in services connected with sanitation, and other aspects of the collective life of the community'.[33] Of course, in this respect she echoed the great nineteenth-century Liberal Joseph Chamberlain. When he was President of the Local Government Board in 1886, Chamberlain authorised municipal schemes of public works (such as street cleaning, street paving, clearing land and building sewage and water works) to relieve the large-scale unemployment in London.

Poor Law Guardians, Emmeline Pankhurst argued, should have greater powers to acquire land, greater freedom to use it and greater freedom to pay those who worked on it. In her view, here was an injustice that could be remedied. She believed that Guardians should purchase or lease land and employ the poor (at reasonable wages) to cultivate it. People, she insisted, wanted to work and urged the Manchester Corporation to employ those out of work on their land at Carrington and Chat Moss. 'Anyone using his eyes,' she argued, 'could see many ways in which the Corporation could find work for those out of employment.' Unfortunately, the Manchester Corporation was unsympathetic to this request. They had, the Mayor informed the Guardians, already a very large number of their own men unemployed in the Cleansing Department and 'were quite at their wits end as to what they could find their men to do'.[34] Moreover, he insisted, the Cleansing Committee had already found employment for approximately 1,400 extra men and argued that it could do no more.

During this particular emergency her husband Richard and Leonard Hall led a deputation of the unemployed – said to be between 325 and 1,000 – to the Poor Law Guardians. Several members of the Board of Guardians objected to their coming because it was considered a serious tax upon their time. Obviously Emmeline spoke in support of their admittance. Eventually, the deputation was allowed to enter and Richard Pankhurst addressed the meeting, arguing, in the same way as his wife, that the Board of Guardians was unequal to the task of grappling with the unemployment issue.

Several Guardians asked Emmeline what she would do with ablebodied men 'who did not like work'. A natural workaholic herself and believing in the value of work to fulfil the human spirit, she replied that men would have to be compelled to work if necessary. Her philosophy of rights and responsibilities meant that men had the right to be offered work but also had the responsibility to take up the opportunities given them. However, she went on to condemn, with some feeling, the economic timidity of the Guardians and proposed that the rates be increased to relieve the distress of the unemployed. Once again she was in the minority. One member suggested that Mrs Pankhurst should apologise to the Board for her emotional outbursts, declaring that she 'had not a monopoly of sympathy with suffering'.[35]

In her short time as Poor Law Guardian, Emmeline Pankhurst was thought to have made an 'incipient revolution'.[36] She undoubtedly helped shape Poor Law policy locally and was involved in projects to prevent and alleviate distress caused by unemployment – arguing against the disfranchisement for those in receipt of relief; increasing the powers of guardians and amending those of the Local Government Board; caring for the elderly, single mothers and deserted and 'feeble-minded' children. Poor Law work did not involve her in quite the same number of 'big issues' which characterised her earlier political career, yet the areas in which she became involved would help define the politics of her later life. Elements of her character too were evident: her dogged persistency and obduracy in the face of what she perceived as parsimonious local government, along with her deeply felt commitment to the poor, would remain with her always.

Emmeline remained at this unpaid official post for over four years until her husband's death in 1898, when a financial crisis allegedly obliged her to resign in favour of paid work as Registrar of Births and Deaths. Political convention meant that Emmeline would be unable to take up her post as Registrar if she remained ILP representative on the same local Board of Guardians. Perhaps, as in the case of so many other women and despite her obvious commitment, she ultimately found her work as Poor Law Guardian too deeply distressing and distinctly unappealing. Personally desolate after the death of Richard, she might have found the harshness of Poor Law work too hard to bear at that moment in her life. In later years she argued that she had been a Guardian in order to prove that women were fit for the rights and responsibilities of citizenship but at the end of it all 'was forced to the conclusion that so far as our enfranchisement was concerned, we had been wasting time'.[37]

THE GENERAL ELECTION 1895

Meanwhile, she continued to help Richard in his fight to become an MP. Both the Pankhursts shared the same faith in the reforming ability of Parliament, so in 1895, one year after joining the ILP and ten years after his last humiliating defeat, Richard Pankhurst fought another general election. This time he stood as ILP candidate for Gorton, an industrially mixed constituency of coal mines and manufacturing, and a former Liberal stronghold, near Manchester. On the face of it Richard Pankhurst seemed to stand a good chance of winning because, as a result of a pact with the Liberals, he stood alone against the Conservatives. The official Liberal candidate for the Gorton division withdrew from the contest, saying: 'Hard things have been at times said by Dr Pankhurst about the Liberal Party and many Liberals have said not less hard things about him, but that he has at heart many of the most cherished objects for which all Liberals are now striving cannot be denied by anyone. Let us forget the unhappy differences between right and left wings of the party of progress and by closing our ranks confront the enemy in such force that victory will be certain all along the line.'[38] Nevertheless, relationships with the Liberals were tense, and, as in 1883, many Liberals declined to vote for a man who refused to compromise his principles to gain their support. As always, Richard Pankhurst was financially embarrassed and could not afford to bear the cost of the election. His new party, the ILP, was equally poor. Consequently, the ILP electoral campaign was severely curtailed by its shortage of funds – at one point it had to rely on chalking footpaths to publicise future meetings.

Again the Pankhursts found themselves on the losing side. Overall, the general election produced a disappointing defeat for the ILP since not one of its twenty-eight candidates was elected. Even Keir Hardie, its founder and leader, was defeated in his West Ham constituency. The outcome proved to be 'the hour of Lancashire Toryism's greatest triumph'.[39] In Gorton some 800 local Liberals voted Tory rather than support Richard Pankhurst, so he only gained 4,261 votes against the Conservatives 5,865. 'How much I owe this fight to Mrs Pankhurst, O! dulcis conjux.'[40] After his defeat she went to help another ILP candidate, Tom Mann, who was standing for the nearby Chorlton seat, and as she drove home alone in her pony and trap she was stoned by a crowd of working-class drunken men in Gorton celebrating the Tory victory. But hostile crowds were not ever to perturb Emmeline Pankhurst unduly; in her future political career she continually faced crowds that were antagonistic to her ideas and methods. The criterion was this: if she believed in the justice of a cause, she would never shrink from proclaiming her arguments – sometimes in situations where her audience was implacable, offensive and even dangerous. Throughout her life, Emmeline's way of putting principles before political pragmatism meant that she would often encounter hostility.

The Pankhursts had moved from the radical fringe of the Liberals to the radical wing of the ILP and, once again, Richard's politics were considered too wild and extreme for the working-class electorate. When the ILP proposed a socialist party programme which was divided into four sections – agricultural, industrial, educational and social, and finally fiscal – the Pankhursts tried to push it further. The preamble to the agricultural policy read: 'That the land being the storehouse of all the essentials of life, ought to be declared and treated as public property, and be so cultivated as to provide the food supply of the people.'[41] At the suggestion of Richard, a State Land Department was set up to implement land nationalisation. From the beginning, the ILP was committed to nationalisation of land and industry. This again was an old Radical-Liberal demand: land reform had long been a middle-class, rather than a working-class, claim because it undermined the foundation of aristocratic wealth,[42] and land nationalisation had been part of the radical programme previously espoused by the Liberal Party. Indeed Chamberlain made the question of land ownership part of his 1885 radical electoral platform.

Undoubtedly, both Pankhursts were leading advocates of the more radical policies of the ILP. When Fred Brocklehurst put forward a motion at the fourth Annual Conference, held in the Mechanics' Hall, Nottingham, on April 6–7th 1896, to change the ILP's name to National Socialist Party, it was supported by Emmeline Pankhurst but defeated by the members. She put forward an alternative suggestion that the sub-title be 'The British Division of the International Socialist Movement', but this too was rejected by a large majority (3 to 1) at the conference.[43] For tactical as much as ideological reasons, the name remained the ILP – it was feared that 'socialism' spelt out might meet with disapproval from prospective voters and thus lead to the unelectability of the newly founded party.

TOWARDS MILITANCY: BOGGART HOLE CLOUGH

The Manchester ILP did score one, albeit small, political victory when they won the right to hold meetings at Boggart Hole Clough, a large open space on the outskirts of the city which had been acquired by Manchester Corporation as a public park. Here too one can see the beginnings of Emmeline's political intransigence, her passionate concern for fairness, her willingness to stand up to injustice whatever the personal cost, her instinctive ability for divining the mood of the moment and her innate propensity for sensing a marketing opportunity. The ILP at this time was a small party with little money and financial backing, so its meetings often took place in squalid rooms or stables or else outdoors in town back streets or parks.[44] The Manchester branch met every Sunday at Boggart Hole Clough. In May 1896 the Chairman of the Parks Committee, probably in a fit of pique because he had been opposed by the ILP in a recent election, prohibited them from holding meetings there. The ILP, which paid no attention to the ban and continued to hold its meetings in the park, found its speakers summonsed before magistrates, convicted and fined. The prosecution argued that the 'gathering of so many people had a tendency to cause damage to the grass and shrubs; and in this case when the keeper remonstrated with those who were trespassing off the footpaths he was hooted ... the literature sold and distributed was scattered over the ground. Some of the language used was of a character calculated to annoy many of the people in the park .... It was a selfish and tyrannical thing for a section of the public to say that they would use the park exactly as they thought fit, to the annoyance of others'[45]

Week after week ILP speakers were prosecuted, fined, refused to pay their penalty and were imprisoned. As a consequence of this action and the increased publicity, meetings got bigger and bigger, swelling from 200 to about 2,000. And not surprisingly, Emmeline Pankhurst was in the middle of it. At first she merely took a supportive role, collecting money for those prosecuted: 'On Sunday 7th June ... Mrs Pankhurst placed her umbrella on the ground and the crowd dropped pennies into it.' Soon she became more involved, speaking at Boggart Hole Clough on May 21st and May 28th 1896, willing to risk imprisonment for the right of free speech by tearing down fences put up to stop the meeting. Like the other protestors, she was summonsed and charged with breaching public order. When she appeared in court on June 26th 1896, she insisted that she was 'fully prepared to take the consequences of her act in speaking at the meeting, and she was aware when she spoke that very likely proceedings would be instituted against her. If the magistrates decided – illegally as she thought – to convict, she would not pay the fine …. She would not be bound over to keep the peace, which she had not broken.'[46] Her friend and comrade Leonard Hall was given one month's imprisonment, whereas her own case was adjourned. She exhibited her usual passion against unequal treatment by uttering an emphatic protest against the lack of a sentence, banging her hand on the dock bar, saying 'I will not be treated like a child'. Her husband, thrilled by her demonstration of courage and political aggression, declared to his friends: 'O isn't she wonderful!'.[47]

A week later, undeterred and all too willing to be a martyr to a cause, she took her two adolescent daughters, Christabel and Sylvia (who collected money towards her defence and for the ILP), with her to Boggart Hole Clough, accompanied by her husband and Keir Hardie. By now crowds estimated at between 25,000 and 40,000 had gathered, and were addressed by several speakers including Emmeline. Boggart Hole Clough was threatening to become a national problem as the conflict between the ILP and the local authorities escalated. Eventually, the Home Secretary, deeply concerned about any threat to public order, refused to sanction the local by-law. Meetings continued to be held and the prosecution case collapsed. But it was to be something of a pyrrhic victory for Emmeline, whose health was badly affected by the episode. In a letter to Tom Mann, Richard noted that 'Mrs Pankhurst is not well. She is … off all public work and its incidental excitement … we are off from Victoria Park to a farmhouse to … go into the country and keep quiet. We are on the move to the farm this week. Mrs Pankhurst's health has never been right since Boggart Hole Clough.'[48] Of course it was here, at Boggart Hole Clough, that she first encountered tactics which would be used to great effect in the suffragette struggle: gaining maximum publicity by refusing to accept legal judgements. Moreover, this was the first time she pushed herself on to the stage of national politics on her own terms rather than in support of her husband.

DEATH OF RICHARD PANKHURST

During this period of local political activity, the Pankhursts' nineteen-year-old marriage ended on July 5th 1898, when Richard Pankhurst died unexpectedly of a perforated stomach ulcer. He was 62, the same age at which Emmeline's father had died six years earlier. She was abroad when Richard died, having taken Christabel, now aged 17, to Geneva to stay with her childhood friend Noémie Rochefort (now Mme Dufaux), and only learned of her husband's death while travelling on a train back to Manchester. Naturally, Emmeline was devastated.

Tributes to her late husband came from all over radical Britain. Richard's life was distinguished by good, if unfulfilled, intentions, and his funeral was lined with mourners all the way from his home in Victoria Park to the cemetery at Brooklands. Representatives from the Manchester Athenaeum, the Portico Library, The Peak District Preservation Society, ILP Federations and many others all attended his funeral.[49] Hundreds of cyclists from the Clarion Cyclists' Club paid their respects. Not surprisingly, the ILP made public statements of condolences and paid numerous tributes to his widow, encapsulated in the following eulogy: 'In him the party lost one of its truest and most devoted members – few know what immense sacrifices he had made for the cause – and one who would, almost certainly, have been returned to the next House of Commons, where his abilities would not only have won for him the admiration of non-Socialists, but would have been of incalculable benefit to his party and to the people of this country. Not merely his personal friends, but all who appreciate the difficulties in our path must regret his untimely death.'[50]

A Memorial Fund was created in recognition of his contribution to the ILP and to help the newly bereaved Pankhurst family now faced with economic crisis, but Emmeline refused to take any money, saying that others were in greater need. After some negotiation the ILP's National Administrative Council agreed to use the fund towards a paid organiser 'whose chief duty should be to prepare constituencies for elections, and to the making of grants of free literature to branches engaged in contests'.[51] A hall was also to be built in his memory. However, although the praise of Richard Pankhurst was overwhelming, members could not be persuaded, or could not afford, to donate the monies required. The NAC only managed to raise £29. 12s 4d, a sum which, even at this time, was not enough to pay for very much. Eventually, when Keir Hardie and Ramsay MacDonald became fund-raisers, enough money was collected to build a Memorial Hall. The 'Pankhurst Hall', which remained the property of a socialist building society, was built in St. James's Road, Hightown, North Salford, and included three lock-up shops, a large hall and various smaller club rooms at a cost of £1,300.[52] On Saturday, October 9th 1900 there was a grand opening of the Pankhurst Memorial Hall: Joseph Nuttal was in the chair for the ceremony, supported on the platform by Emmeline Pankhurst, her son and three daughters, Mr and Mrs Bruce Glasier and Tom Cook.[53] On November 25th 1900 Keir Hardie delivered the inaugural lecture at the Pankhurst Memorial Hall in honour of his former comrade.

Richard's death had several consequences for Emmeline. For many middle-class women, the coincidence of widowhood and middle age brought a modicum of financial independence, freedom from children and the opportunity to develop their own personal interests. Richard Pankhurst's death, however, both constrained and liberated her simultaneously. Her haven of affection and stability had gone. Yet even when he was employed as a barrister Richard had never earned vast amounts of money. Moreover, he had been continually in debt. And so, in 1899, shortly after her husband's death, she moved from Daisy Bank to 62 Nelson Street, a much smaller and less grand house. Her political activities were also constrained because she had to make a living – her children, now aged respectively 18, 16, 13 and 11, were all still economically dependent on her. For the first time in her life she took a paid job, as Registrar of Marriages, Births and Deaths. Perhaps most challenging of all, with her political mentor gone she would have to rely entirely on her own judgements and make her own way in the political world.

EDUCATION

After Richard's death, Emmeline continued to work for good causes. Of course, politics was in every fibre of her being so although newly widowed and for the first time engaged in full-time paid work, she was drawn to political action. After several attempts, she was elected in 1900 as the ILP representative for the Manchester School Board. Thirty years earlier, in 1870, William Forster, Quaker and Vice-President of Gladstone's first Liberal administration, had introduced a new Education Act which provided secular elementary education for all children between the ages of 5 and 13 not already provided for by the religious denominational schools already in existence. Local School Boards were set up to administer this Act and to build schools when and where needed. The Manchester Board was the first to be elected in England and was one of the largest and most influential in the country. These School Boards gave women new opportunities to become involved in local politics, both as voters and Board members.[54]

Provincial School Boards were elected under a unique system of cumulative voting, whereby each voter had the same number of votes as there were seats on the School Board and could allocate all their votes for one candidate or split them as they wished. In Manchester each elector had up to fifteen votes which could, in principle, all be given to one candidate[55] – this enabled women to be elected more easily since they could draw upon the votes of feminists and other women. In addition, by the mid-1870s most School Boards were run on party lines so that in places like Manchester, which had a high Liberal vote, Liberal women would find themselves on the School Board. And so could ILP candidates. There is some confusion over when Emmeline Pankhurst was actually selected as an ILP candidate, but the *Clarion* establishes that she was selected in September 1894 at a meeting of the United Labour Party School Board Election Committee.[56] (As it turned out, all ILP members finished at the bottom of the Manchester poll, although Emmeline Pankhurst secured some 26,644 votes.) Although it was an unremunerated post with a heavy workload, she kept on trying to be elected to the School Board, once more reflecting her persistent character. The School Board had a number of leading Liberal feminists serving on its Committee and her failure was certainly not due to misogynistic tendencies of the School Board or antagonism towards Emmeline Pankhurst's radical and feminist politics. Lydia Becker, national organiser of women's suffrage, was the first woman elected on to the Manchester Board and remained an active member for almost twenty years. Other Liberal women were also elected: Rachel Scott, wife of C.P. Scott, editor of the Liberal paper *The Manchester Guardian*, served on the

Board for six years until 1896, when Mary Dendy took her place. Emmeline Pankhurst's problem in the Manchester constituency was that she was a member of the ILP rather than a Liberal.

Eventually she succeeded. In the elections of the School Board for the City of Manchester, held on 17 November 1900, she stood as a United Educational (a 'union' of the ILP, Trades' Council and the United Educational Party). Fifteen members were returned, including Emmeline Pankhurst, 'widow and registrar of births and deaths', who was elected with 34,502 votes.[57] She was never an educationalist in the sense of Mary Dendy or Emily Davies, yet she became immersed in managing and improving schools within her district, and in extending the remit of the School Board beyond that of the formal curriculum. Her relentless energy and appetite for hard work were now put to use in the field of education. Indeed, she remained as dynamic as ever, involving herself in a range of activities designed to promote the education of the working-class youth.

Like many of her contemporaries, she equated a healthy mind with a healthy body, something which could only be achieved by exercise and diet. She was a member of the sub-committee for the 'systematic instruction in physical exercise' of children in Board Schools, promoting PE in schools and making sure that halls and playgrounds were fully utilised. As a member of the Sanitary Sub-committee she helped appoint a medical officer, at an annual salary of £250 per annum, to instruct senior girls on how to feed babies, and to teach them the importance of cleanliness (small towels were provided by some schools for scholars).[58] To make sure that the newly appointed officer promoted their policies, she helped devise a schedule of duties to be followed.[59] The Manchester Sub-committee also recommended that pupil teachers and senior girls were given cookery lessons as well as the usual academic work.[60] In addition, Emmeline Pankhurst, concerned that school pupils were underfed and therefore could not concentrate on school work, belonged to the 'Tending and Feeding of Children Sub-committee'.

Not surprisingly, given her work with 'feeble-minded' paupers as Poor Law Guardian, she worked hard to improve the education of other school-aged children perceived to be 'feeble-minded'. In March 1901, when two of the special schools, at Embden Street, Hulme, and Hague Street, Newton Heath, were in the final stages of completion,[61] Emmeline Pankhurst, Mary Dendy and others met as part of the Feeble-minded Children Sub-committee to consider the appointment of staff. These staff were well paid and included a Miss June B. Dickens, who was appointed as the first superintendent at £175 per annum (the same amount as an inspector of schools received, a good wage for a middle-class woman at the time), an experienced headmistress with a salary of £150 p.a. and assistant teachers. Salaries were most likely higher than the national average in order to attract the best staff and the number of children in each school was kept small – Embden Street accommodating just over 40 and Hague Street accommodating 80, compared to most schools which accommodated well over 1,000 pupils – probably in order to give specialist treatment to particularly disadvantaged children.

Emmeline Pankhurst voted for the abolition of fees in all elementary schools. Elementary education was made compulsory for all pupils up to the age of 10 in 1876 and free for those attending Board Schools in 1891. Not all schools in Manchester were free, since a large number of children attended the charity schools which still charged fees. The system in Manchester meant 'that the upper clerks and warehousemen in one district, and well paid artisans in another, and the semi-rural parents in Moston and Clayton paid no fees whatever, whilst in some of the schools in Hulme, fringe of Stretford Road in Harpurhey, Oldham Road and near London Road fees were still exacted.'[62] This resulted in an anomaly whereby poorer working-class parents had to contribute towards the cost of their children's education, whereas the wealthier skilled workers did not have to pay. Eventually, on January 5th 1903, all fees were abolished in elementary schools.

The idea of extending education beyond elementary-school level was one that appealed to Emmeline, and she was successful in using her influence within the School Board Committee structure to achieve this. Under the 1870 Act children were entitled to elementary education until the age of 10 (increased in 1893 to 11 and in 1899 to 12), but after the age of 12 there was no responsibility for any authority to provide education. In practice, the Manchester School Board used money from the rates and grants from government to provide what was virtually a secondary education within the elementary school structure. Technically, this was illegal since the 1870 Act had only established that elementary education could be supported from the rates, a decision confirmed by the Cockerton Judgement of 1901, which ruled that elementary schools which provided education to children older than 12 were acting illegally. Emmeline condemned this and moved a resolution at the ILP Conference in 1901 that 'legislation securing for school boards the right of continuing and developing these classes and schools is required immediately.'[63] The Manchester City School Board agreed with her sentiments and produced a petition in support of higher elementary education.

Emmeline was not a member of the Finance Committee (which tended to concern itself with teachers' salaries and petty cash), but she did become involved in financial affairs when there were perceived injustices. It was not surprising that, given her principles, she tried to promote women. On February 29th 1904 she, along with Eva Gore-Booth, decided that boy and girl pupil teachers would be paid *equal* salaries. She also supported the appointment of a woman inspector for infant schools whose salary would be in the region of £200 per annum. When the Board of Education contracted out some of its work, she expressed concern that the contractors might be exploiting their employees. She seconded a resolution that firms contracting for or doing the Board's work must pay its workers a standard wage and must observe the hours of work recognised by 'the local organised bodies of workers'. In order to stop possible bribery and corruption she persuaded the rest of the Board that no member should receive a gratuity from a contractor (or would-be contractor).[64]

Technically she was elected for a term of three years, but when School Boards were abolished under the 1902 Education Act she lost her seat. Emmeline Pankhurst protested against the new law at the ILP Conference in 1902, where she was delegate for Chorlton. She condemned the Act because elementary education control passed to the town and county council rather than the elected School Board and because it deprived women of the right to be elected. At the tenth Annual Conference of the ILP she seconded a resolution which criticised the Act because it subsidised denominational education and deprived women of their right to be directly elected.[65] Unlike many of her formal proposals, this one was carried by the conference.

Now that she was out of a post, Emmeline, together with the previous School Board members, requested that the clerk of the Manchester School Board convene a special meeting on March 23rd 1903 to ask that she and other officers be co-opted on to the Education Committee.

Fortunately, the 1902 Act made it mandatory to have at least two women members on the new Education Committees, thus making it possible for the Manchester School Board to include her. This they did and four women members – Eva Gore-Booth, Sara Burstall, Mary Dendy and Emmeline Pankhurst – were duly co-opted. She represented the Manchester and Salford Trades Council on the Manchester Education Committee until 1904, when she 'resigned to devote all her time to Women's Suffrage'.[66]

Even after her resignation from the LEA, Emmeline continued to take an interest in the health of school children. She was concerned that young children were not eating sufficient food and recognised the futility of attempting to educate underfed pupils. Her autobiography suggests that she was in favour of women teachers 'spending their slender salaries to provide regular dinners for destitute children'[67] but at the time she opposed charity because it degraded the children who were offered it. At a Manchester Central Branch of the ILP on September 5th 1905 she put forward a resolution saying: 'That this branch of the ILP condemn the scheme issued by the Manchester Education Committee for the feeding of necessitous school children, as it would put upon them the stigma of pauperism.'[68] Instead she suggested that school restaurants be established so that working-class children could buy breakfast and lunch.[69]

CONCLUSION

It may be impossible to determine the exact genesis of Emmeline Pankhurst's ideas. Nonetheless, one can discern some of the major elements which formed her later beliefs: her sympathies with eugenics and her continuing commitment to working-class women remained strong personal threads, both in her work as Poor Law Guardian and as a member of Manchester School Board. Her basic tenets remained the same. Even though she was not active in suffrage, she signalled her continuing commitment to the cause by putting forward suffrage proposals at ILP conferences.

This period was one in which she was able to implement some of her radical ideas. In so doing, she gained valuable political experience in a number of fields and her work, as with many other women, helped to shape the structure of local politics in Manchester. All her various committee work, both as Poor Law Guardian and as education representative, might have enabled her to develop the skills to argue her cause, but the frustrations experienced while doing so might well have contributed to her antagonism towards any kind of discussion which might inhibit action. Nonetheless, her willingness to be a Guardian and to work on the Manchester School Board show a pragmatic and practical response towards the problems of the poor. Emmeline preferred to give practical help rather than issue ideological missives. As Richard's electoral assistant, she continued to hone her electioneering skills, having reinforced at the same time the understanding that politics was a brutal business. At Boggart Hole Clough, according to her daughter Sylvia, she learned her skills in public speaking, hesitant at first but increasing in confidence, thus beginning her career as a charismatically poised woman. Here, she showed an inner compulsion to sacrifice her freedom to uphold democracy, exhibiting the same political fearlessness that would characterise her later political life. Whatever the outcome, Emmeline did not moderate her rhetoric to fit the occasion, as ever remaining uncompromising in her beliefs.

During this period, Emmeline defined herself as a socialist woman. Certainly, she was a very active ILP member, regularly attending committee meetings, being elected to the Executive and producing the *ILP News*. Emmeline may have acted as ILP representative on a number of local bodies but many of her values (e.g. her belief in rights and responsibilities, her ideas about the 'deserving' poor, her support for land reformation, her commitment to free speech, her advancement of education and her continuing demands for women's suffrage) were as much Liberal principles as socialist ones. Socialism, however, was more attractive to Emmeline because it practised what Liberalism preached.

Undoubtedly, Emmeline worked hard at whatever she did. She had that touch of obsession necessary to deliver results, demonstrating the indefatigable energy which would become her trademark. What is striking is the sheer busyness of her life, running her home, looking after the children, supporting Richard, visiting the workhouse, campaigning for justice and attending a multitude of meetings. It was an exhilarating, if somewhat exhausting, introduction to politics. The skills developed in one area of her life were later utilised in others. For example, the skills learnt in campaigning and local politics were later adapted to suffrage work. She was qualified for the job of leading what was to become one of the most famous women's organisations by virtue of the personal and political experience gained in her involvement at grass-roots level in Manchester.

Part II

THE SUFFRAGETTE STORY
1903–14

4

SUFFRAGETTE BEGINNINGS
1903–07

INTRODUCTION

In October 1903 Emmeline Pankhurst and her daughters founded the all-female Women's Social and Political Union (WSPU) at their house in Nelson Street, Manchester. Six other women, including Pattie Hall (the wife of Leonard Hall, who had been arrested with Emmeline at Boggart Hole Clough), were invited to join them. Years later Emmeline Pankhurst told Pattie Hall's daughter that her dining-room table bore the indelible marks of the 'Votes for Women' placard which they had made and put up outside her home.

By now she had had an impressive training in public affairs. Widowed for five years and with her children more or less grown up, she was to devote the years between 1903 and 1914 to women's suffrage. Her previous political experience, her conspicuous and considerable dedication and her enormous vitality were all harnessed to rejuvenate and revitalise the movement. She was to break the mould of women's politics: in an age of suffragist moderation she advocated political extremism and urgency. In so doing, she was to tower over the reawakening of the suffrage movement, especially when her frequent challenges to authority brought intense publicity and thus generated great public interest. Her sheer personal magnetism, her eloquence and her militancy all contributed to her growing iconic status.

Emmeline Pankhurst wanted to cast off the Liberal image of women's suffrage, to reverse the alleged decades of suffrage defeat and turn the WSPU into a viable political machine. Jealous of Christabel's developing friendship with Esther Roper and Eva Gore-Booth and spurred on by the fact that they had just founded the Lancashire and Cheshire Women Textile and Other Workers Representation Committee, she felt prompted to form her own organisation. In her autobiography she argued that she wished to keep the WSPU independent and 'free from any party affiliation'.[1] In effect, this statement is little more than historical rhetoric since the early WSPU was not just sympathetic to the newly emerging Labour Party but almost an offshoot of it.[2] In some ways she hoped to emulate the relationship between the National Union of Women's Suffrage Societies (NUWSS) and the Liberal Party. Female Liberals dominated the NUWSS. Its leader, Millicent Fawcett, was the wife of a Liberal cabinet minister. Moreover, the inter-locking membership of the NUWSS and the Women's Liberal Federation meant that Liberal candidates who favoured women's suffrage always had volunteers to canvass for them and work hard to secure their election.[3] In return, these Liberal MPs promoted women's suffrage in the House of Commons.

Emmeline, who had long ceased to be a member of the Liberal Party, aimed to forge a similar alliance between the WSPU and the Labour Party. Keir Hardie had just been returned to Parliament, so there was a renewed optimism about the future of parliamentary socialism and women's suffrage – especially when she drafted a suffrage resolution that Keir Hardie introduced in Parliament. Initially, the WSPU received both moral and financial support from Labour. The WSPU, modelled on the working-class socialist movement, took women's suffrage out of the drawing rooms and on to the streets to campaign among the north of England factory workers. In the early years the links between the WSPU and the Labour Party seemed robust, with the two organisations working in unison. Teresa Billington, a founder member of the WSPU, was a paid organiser for Labour and during the 1905 Manchester municipal elections canvassed female electors to vote for the party. In turn, Emmeline helped Teresa Billington by speaking at all-women meetings, focusing on issues generally regarded as female concerns, such as sanitation, the feeding of school children and housing.[4]

By the time the WSPU emerged on the political scene, the old disagreements over which group of women should obtain the vote had been resolved. They, as with the other suffrage groups, campaigned for a limited franchise, demanding votes for women on the same terms as men possessed them.[5] Initially, what distinguished the WSPU from other societies was that it was an all-female organisation. It has been assumed by a number of historians that the decision to exclude men laid the foundations for a sex war.[6] But Emmeline was never anti-male: 'we are not fighting against men, but *for* women ... our first and greatest rule is – to be good to other women.'[7] Repeatedly, she urged unity, rather than class divisiveness, for women. In her view, gender should and must override class differences. She believed there was a need for an autonomous, separate organisation of women, which the WSPU, a female organisation, provided. It was her commitment to women, rather than her antagonism towards men and male politics, which fuelled her political thinking in these years.

WHY EMMELINE PANKHURST WANTED THE VOTE

Emmeline Pankhurst was not much of a political theorist, and the reasons why she wanted the vote mirrored those of other suffragists. Her reasoning, however, was never abstract since the arguments she put forward became the political strategies of the WSPU. She was a democratic socialist, not a Marxist, so wanted women to be part of the constitutional process rather than overthrow Parliament by revolution. She saw the vote as an inalienable right, a passport to citizenship and civilisation and the cornerstone of a parliamentary system. Democracy, she argued, did not exist in Britain since one half of humanity was excluded from it. Government of the people, by the people and for the people, she insisted, was 'only for male consumption; half of the people were entirely ignored'.[8] Suffrage activists like Emmeline criticised the fact that women had been consistently excluded from each of the franchise reform acts of 1832, 1867 and 1884. At the time, all men who paid rates and taxes, who were owners, occupiers, lodgers or had a service or university franchise (i.e. two-thirds of adult males), possessed the vote. The rest of the male population – and all women – were denied the franchise. It was estimated that if women obtained the vote on the same terms as men, approximately a million-and-a-quarter women would be able to vote with the seven-and-a-half million men who were already franchised.

Emmeline considered it inappropriate to claim that Britain had a representative government when the majority of the population was disenfranchised on the grounds of gender. In her view, Britain had an unjust and unbalanced political system. According to her, and indeed many other suffragists, women had all the duties and none of the rights associated with democracy.[9] It was considered unfair that women had to obey laws and pay taxes equally with men, yet had no voice in deciding what those laws and taxes should be. Women were taxed without being represented and taxation without representation she considered tyranny. Moreover, Emmeline objected to the fact that women, who paid taxes and local rates, were classed alongside criminals and lunatics, who were disenfranchised for reasons of either punishment or mental incapacity. So members like Dora Montefiore refused to pay taxes and barricaded themselves into their homes when bailiffs came to sequester their goods. Denied access to democracy, Emmeline felt justified in taking more direct action.

Throughout her life she argued not only for the vote itself but also for the use to which it could be put. Democracy, Emmeline believed, could effect radical change. Intellectually, she did not originate any new argument in support of votes for women and her reasoning was identical to that of other suffragists. For her the vote was 'first of all, a symbol, secondly a safeguard, and thirdly an instrument'. It was 'a symbol of freedom, a symbol of citizenship, a symbol of liberty',[10] which safeguarded those self-same liberties as well as helping to facilitate social change. It was, to her thinking, a political, moral, social and economic imperative. She argued that women should have the vote so that women's point of view could be put forward in Parliament, because 'no race or class or sex can have its interest properly safeguarded in the legislature of a country unless it is represented by direct suffrage.'[11] She, like other suffrage supporters, believed that under a representative government the interests of any non-represented group were likely to be neglected. At the beginning of the nineteenth century the vote had been less significant than patronage in parliamentary politics: the vast majority of the population were without the vote and the minority of those enfranchised had little real influence on government thinking. By the time Emmeline was active in the suffrage movement, suffragists viewed the vote as a powerful tool to transform the lives of women. All too often, as she argued, women's needs were not examined since governments tended to the demands of those who had the vote. She went further: the group that held political power – in other words men – made laws favourable to themselves and neglected the interests of those without power, including women. She was particularly concerned with family law. Even at the start of the twentieth century, women still suffered from legislative inequality within marriage, yet if they wanted to divorce their husbands it was virtually impossible to do so. Emmeline Pankhurst wanted equal marital rights for women. Moreover, she expressed concern that married women were denied full parental control over their children because husbands decided the future of their children, where they should live, how they should live, how they should be educated and what religion they should profess. Single mothers, she believed, were no better off, because they were blamed for their indiscretions, held solely responsible for the upbringing of their child and punished if their child was neglected. Unjust laws, she argued, continued because men had no need to consult women or to defer to their opinions.

Politics and economics were thought to go hand in hand. Emmeline Pankhurst, often criticised by historians for neglecting the interests of the working class once she became immersed in the WSPU, in fact replaced a class perspective with a gender one. Insisting that female identity superseded that of class, she linked 'self-supporting' women of all classes together under the umbrella of gender inequalities. As long as women had no political status, she argued, they would never earn enough. Women, whatever their class background, were the worst-paid group of workers, whose conditions were also the poorest. She contrasted the experience of voteless women workers with enfranchised miners who had successfully achieved an eight-hour day; in contrast, sweated women workers and professional women received nothing. She drew comparisons between the injustices faced by all women. Working-class women continued to work for long hours and low wages in inhumane conditions, whereas professional women found it difficult to obtain posts after they had qualified. Probably mindful that her daughter Sylvia had suffered from sex discrimination at the College of Arts, she referred to the fact that women never obtained paid posts there: 'All the professorships, all the well-paid posts in the colleges and Universities are given to men.'[12] The more important and lucrative positions were usually barred to women and opportunities for public service denied them. She believed that, empowered by the vote, women might gain access to jobs as inspectors of prisons, workhouses and factories, where few, if any, women worked. Equal pay, she believed, might be a reality for women teachers once the vote had been won. 'You see what the vote will do. You see what political power will do .... It is the political key that is needed to unlock the door,'[13] she argued.

Emmeline also objected to the way in which Parliament could pass laws which affected women directly, yet women had no political redress if they disagreed with them. When the leading trade unionist and Labour MP John Burns tried to prevent married women from working in factories (ostensibly to stop infant mortality), she argued strongly against him. She claimed that Lancashire cotton workers were much better off financially than unemployed workers or sweated trade workers and home-workers who earned little and worked long hours. Well-paid workers, she asserted, were able to provide all kinds of benefits for their families which resulted in better health all round. 'Infant mortality and physical degeneration were not found in the homes of the well-paid factory operatives,' she maintained. Instead, they were 'found in the home of the slum dweller, the home of the casual labourer, where the mother does not go out to work but where there is never sufficient income to provide proper food for the child after it is born.'[14]

Until the recent work of feminist historians, most history texts ignored the emphasis Emmeline Pankhurst placed on sex and morality or else have used it as an excuse to ridicule the suffragettes. However, Emmeline took pains to position women's franchise within the wider context of sexual politics and took the question of sexuality very earnestly indeed. For her, the vote was as much a tool for improving men's sexual morality as it was for improving women's working conditions. She wanted the vote to cleanse the perceived corruption of public life and ensure that men and women adhered to the same moral principles. This, in turn, would go some way towards eliminating venereal disease. She confidently assumed that votes for women were necessary to eliminate the sexual double standard whereby it was acceptable for men, but not women, to have sex outside marriage. When she was a Poor Law Guardian, the increasing number of single mothers who were dependent on the state because men refused to marry them or pay them maintenance had distressed her. Years later she argued that one of the things that made her a militant after nearly thirty years of constitutional effort was her experience as a Registrar of Births and Deaths in Manchester.

She claimed that whenever a woman came to register her baby's death with the death certificate sealed in an envelope, it was invariably because the baby had died of inherited syphilis. In her view, there was a conspiracy between doctors and husbands who covered up the facts so that these women did not know the true cause of their babies' death.[15] Later, she added white slavery, that is international prostitution, to the list of reasons why women needed to be enfranchised. She believed that prostitution itself was slavery and condemned the government for being one of the biggest white slave traders in existence since it encouraged prostitution in India and other places in which the British armed forces were stationed. Morality, she believed, was important to the nation. 'We women must realise our importance to the race. What we are the race will be. We, the mothers of the race, must be free in order that we may be the mothers of a free people.'[16]

Emmeline Pankhurst equated inequality and disenfranchisement with prostitution. To her thinking, working-class women were especially susceptible to prostitution because of their economic vulnerability. In private, she was most circumspect about her own sexuality. Rhetta Dorr claimed that she 'could never get her to talk about any phase of women's sex nature. The subject repelled her. She had a strong puritan streak and thought the only solution of the social evil was the conversion of men to complete celibacy outside marriage.'[17] In public, however, she was very outspoken. Concern for sexual morality within the WSPU has often been attributed to her daughter, Christabel, whose insistence on Chastity for Men is well known. Yet it was Emmeline who had first raised it as an issue. Throughout her life, from her participation in the WFrL, through to her work as Poor Law Guardian and Registrar and finally in the WSPU campaign, she had continually challenged the double standard of morality existing within Britain at the time. As time went on, Emmeline became increasingly convinced of the prevalence of white slavery, which could only be eradicated once women were enfranchised.

TOWARDS MILITANCY

For the first two years of its existence, the WSPU worked in the north of England. It had a tiny membership who spent their time speaking to radical societies and trade union meetings largely composed of working-class women. Christabel and Sylvia Pankhurst, Annie Kenney and Hannah Mitchell were all dubbed 'Mrs Pankhurst's suffrage missionaries' – they and Emmeline travelled widely in the north of England in these years, gradually building up support for women's suffrage. Yet, even at this time, there were the first intimations of militancy. On suffrage deputations Emmeline often embarrassed other suffragists by her direct questioning of ministers.

In 1905 the tactics of a new movement began to emerge. On May 12th 1905 Emmeline travelled down to London with Elizabeth Wolstenholme-Elmy to hear a private member's bill on women's suffrage put forward by a sympathetic Liberal MP. When the bill was 'talked out' by a Roadway Lighting Bill, she held an impromptu protest meeting and signed a resolution condemning Parliament for its lack of action. This, according to Emmeline Pankhurst, was the start of the militant campaign. Yet it was the action of her daughter, Christabel, which has captured public and historical attention, when Christabel famously interrupted a Liberal election meeting in October, it is said to have marked an important turning point that heralded a new and distinct form of political tactics. Although not present at the meeting, Emmeline was very aware of what was about to happen. She spoke later of Christabel and Annie Kenney 'going to a great Liberal demonstration in the Free Trade Hall, Manchester, of two girls with a little banner, made on my dining-room table, with the inscription "Votes for Women"'.[18]

At this meeting Christabel and Annie Kenney interrupted Sir Edward Grey by asking: 'Will the Liberal Government give votes to women?' When their question was ignored, the two young women unfurled their home-made banner. The atmosphere in the hall must have been electric at this point since hostile interruptions, especially from women, at this type of political meeting, packed with sympathisers, were rare. After a promise that an answer to their question would be given later, the two women waited patiently. When it was evident that Edward Grey would not respond, Christabel Pankhurst and Annie Kenney asked their question again, only to be unceremoniously thrown out of the meeting. Outside the Free Trade Hall police officers and stewards surrounded the two women, whereupon Christabel spat in the face of a policeman who was restraining her. This, a 'technical assault', meant that she was arrested, charged with assaulting a police officer and put on trial. In court both she and Annie Kenney refused to pay the magistrate's fine and were duly imprisoned. According to Christabel, her mother's face was 'drawn and cold' when she was informed.[19] In her own autobiography, Emmeline Pankhurst stated that she offered to pay Christabel's fine so that she could return home but her daughter refused. *The Times* reported that she was 'proud that her daughter had taken so courageous a stand'. Certainly, she accepted the responsibility for a militant policy, although her official, and paid, post as Registrar was threatened.

These incidents were the beginning of a new political tactic of militancy. Unsympathetic observers have viewed militancy humorously or else sought explanations within a psychological framework of madness and abnormality. Militancy, for some anti-suffragists, was seen as a reflection of the widespread instability of women and, more particularly, of fanatical and hysterical women like Emmeline Pankhurst. Hence, to them, it was proof that women should not be allowed to vote. The first historians to write about the suffragettes agreed with the anti-suffragists, emphasised the psychological weakness of the suffragettes and decried militancy as the action of a few demented spinsters spurred on by the now notorious widow. George Dangerfield, for example, writes comically about women:

> it is almost impossible to write the story of the Woman's Rebellion without admitting certain elements of brutal comedy. From the spectacle of women attacking men there rises an outrageous, an unprincipled laughter. And when a scene as ordinary as English politics is suddenly disturbed with the swish of long skirts, the violent assault of feathered hats, the impenetrable, advancing phalanx of corseted bosoms ... then the amazing, the ludicrous appearance of the whole thing is almost irresistible.[20]

More recently, however, historians have become critical of this interpretation and suggest that militancy was a rational response to male intransigence. Brian Harrison, who offers a more sympathetic interpretation, claims that militancy was a temporary tactical necessity born of the failure of legal and peaceful methods. Even so, Harrison is not averse to trivialising the women's struggle by arguing that it more 'closely resembles the schoolgirls' surreptitious breaking of the rules when the headmistress is away than the revolutionary's contemptuous and frontal challenge to the established order'.[21] Radical feminist historians, such as

Jane Marcus, view suffragette violence quite differently. For them, violent behaviour challenged male supremacy, thus establishing Emmeline Pankhurst as not only heroic but as a foremother of modern feminism.

One of the most provocative, and sophisticated, explanations for militancy is put forward by Sandra Stanley Holton, who suggests that militancy cannot be explained adequately by reference to individual psychological disorders, to different campaign tactics, styles of organisation or to feminist heroism.[22] In her view, Emmeline Pankhurst's militancy was informed by an awareness of her historical legacy, an understanding of social and political change and her moral philosophy. Sandra Holton asserts that the suffragette leader's world vision, inspired by reading Carlyle on the French Revolution, was revolutionary in its scope – in marked contrast to Millicent Fawcett's, who, as leader of the constitutionalist wing, believed in evolutionary progress. This is an attractive proposition, but throughout her life Emmeline remained a radical in the old tradition, believing in evolutionary rather than revolutionary advance. Her fondness for Carlyle was inspired by her admiration of France's struggle against the *ancien régime* rather than an intrinsic commitment to revolutionary politics. It is within the context of her commitment to parliamentary democracy rather than revolutionary idealism that her militancy must be placed. She believed in the classic Liberal principle that citizens were entitled to break the law, if they were not allowed to make it. Indeed, Emmeline Pankhurst was never a starry-eyed romantic who mythologised revolution but a keenly attuned pragmatist with an instinctive approach to politics who believed that those who were disenfranchised had every right to break the law in their fight for parliamentary reform.

Moreover, Emmeline Pankhurst was a political opportunist. She was swift to capitalise on events and had an impressive ability to create a separate autonomous women's organisation for which militancy was the defining characteristic. Her speeches, a mixture of historical references and emotional justifications, increasingly referred to the need for violent action. Early on in the suffragette campaign she declared that since the government was reluctant to give women the vote voluntarily, it must be forced to do so. Politicians, she argued, only ever conceded to massive public pressure or to violence – rational arguments left them unmoved. Women, she insisted, had been patient for too long. The militant methods of the WSPU were first adopted after fifty years of persuasion and appeal by other suffrage societies to which politicians had allegedly turned a deaf ear. She justified militancy by the fact that she had tried all other available means but had failed to secure justice. She was by nature a law-abiding person, she maintained, who hated violence and disorder, but there was no other way for her movement to progress.[23] Since 1869 various bills and resolutions which would have enfranchised a number of women had been put before the House of Commons. Debates had taken place in 1870, 1871, 1872, 1875, 1876, 1877, 1878, 1879, 1883, 1884, 1886, 1892, 1897, and in 1904. Three suffrage bills – in 1870, in 1886 and in 1897 – had passed their second reading. During the years when there was no debate, supporters had either been unable to secure a day, or their day was taken up by government business, or by holidays, or the bill or resolution had been blocked, postponed or crowded out. Since 1886 the majority of MPs had been in favour of women's suffrage but in practice it had not been achieved. Therefore Emmeline thought it was time to act. Of course, with historical hindsight, one can see that she misread the situation. As historians have pointed out, suffrage reform had made progress since the midnineteenth century with support steadily building up in the House of Commons. By the end of the century the majority of MPs voted in support of women's suffrage bills, and it just seemed a matter of time before votes for women were gained.[24] Emmeline Pankhurst, however, did not care to wait; she was, to paraphrase Lord Randolph Churchill, an older woman in a hurry. She wanted to speed up what was seen to be the inevitable.

Militancy was justified because it achieved results. Each action was designed to catch press attention and thereby generate a high public profile and the publicity necessary to increase interest in the suffrage movement. The success of pressure groups that had attained their goals through violence convinced her that women's suffrage would only be obtained through similar action. In her speeches she maintained that each extension of the male franchise had been preceded by violence. Drawing on historical examples of the unlawful exercise of physical force, she justified her tactics and identified the suffragettes with past revolutionary and resistance heroes. She told audiences how just before 1832, when middle-class men were enfranchised, half the city of Bristol was burned down in a single night in protest; how the 1867 Reform Act, which enfranchised working men, was preceded by rioting and unrest; how the last male franchise reform in 1884, which enfranchised the agricultural labourer, was marked by threats of civil disorder. In addition, she drew comparisons between the tactics of the suffragettes and those of the Ulster Unionists, whose actions, seen to go unchecked and unpunished even when it involved the loss of human life, were successful in stopping the move towards Irish Home Rule. However, these political comparisons were inapt since it is recognised that force and the threat of force had very little to do with the 1867 and even less with the 1884 franchise reforms. Moreover, those who opposed Irish Home Rule had the vote and would therefore be listened to by Parliament.

Undoubtedly, the militancy of Christabel Pankhurst and Annie Kenney broke the press silence on votes for women. Their protest led to a staggering and unprecedented rise in the membership of all suffrage societies and produced a flush of new suffrage organisations and great financial success for the WSPU. One act of militancy had led to immense publicity that over forty years of peaceful campaigning had failed to achieve. Not surprisingly, Emmeline Pankhurst continued these innovative strategies and promoted militancy at every opportunity.

CONSTITUTIONAL MILITANCY

On December 4th 1905 the Liberal leader Campbell-Bannerman became Prime Minister. A general election was called for January 1906 and the party machinery swung into action. Emmeline Pankhurst and the WSPU just wanted confirmation as to whether – or not – the Liberal Party would support votes for women when in office. In the election campaign that year Liberal ministers were continually questioned about whether or not they would grant votes for women, an answer to which the government steadfastly refused to give. Consequently, the leading Liberals, Winston Churchill (Liberal candidate for NorthWest Manchester), Asquith and Campbell-Bannerman, all had meetings interrupted by WSPU activists. Meanwhile, Emmeline and Annie Kenney canvassed in Merthyr Tydfil in support of the candidacy of Keir Hardie, who, when he won the seat, attributed his success to the efforts made by Emmeline Pankhurst on his behalf.

In 1906, after twenty years of Conservative rule, the Liberals won a landslide victory and had, according to Emmeline, every opportunity to give votes to women, had they wished to do so. Annie Kenney was sent to lodge with Sylvia Pankhurst and to 'rouse London' in support of women's suffrage. Annie Kenney and Sylvia hired Caxton Hall for a meeting to coincide with the opening of Parliament and began campaigning among the working-class women in London's East End. On February 19th 1906 Parliament opened, and so did the meeting at Caxton Hall. Hundreds of women from the East End mixed with members of the old radical elite, only to hear that women's suffrage had not even been mentioned in the King's Speech, a speech that traditionally mapped out the policies of the new Parliament. Emmeline Pankhurst, who had travelled down from Manchester to be at Caxton Hall, quickly took charge, condemned the government for its lack of support for votes for women and suggested that the meeting lobby the House of Commons. This day marked the start of new forms of action and counter-action, as hundreds of women approached the Strangers' Entrance of the House of Commons to lobby their MPs, only to be prohibited from entering by the police. Eventually, two relays, each consisting of approximately twenty women, were admitted into the Lobby, where they were met by a number of MPs, all of whom refused to pledge support for women's suffrage. This may have constituted failure in many eyes, yet Emmeline Pankhurst viewed the episode as a success in that it had firmly established WSPU militancy. She insisted that a more militant attitude had to be adopted if votes for women were to be achieved.

As with the Manchester Free Trade Hall meeting, the Lobby incident brought greater publicity and, equally importantly, an increase in membership. Two of the more important recruits of that period were Emmeline Pethick-Lawrence, who was to become treasurer of the WSPU, and her husband Frederick, who was allowed to become an ex-officio member. Soon the WSPU moved from its base in Sylvia Pankhurst's studio to Clement's Inn, the Strand, largely because of the munificence of the Pethick-Lawrences. Emmeline Pankhurst, still living in Manchester and still employed as Registrar, encouraged members to sustain their London campaign by organising deputations to the Prime Minister and various other ministers. Her visits to London multiplied. On April 4th 1906 she was present at a Labour Party dinner in the House of Commons; on 25th April she was in the House of Commons when Keir Hardie presented her draft of the women's suffrage resolution; and on May 19th she attended a thousand-strong demonstration and was part of a deputation to Campbell-Bannerman. On this occasion, suffrage groups and representatives from various trade unions came from all over Britain. It was the beginning of a new style of demonstration, with many women dressed up in their working clothes, mothers carrying their children and women representatives from all over the world. In October that year she led yet another deputation to Parliament, where her daughter Adela and several other women were arrested for trying to make speeches in the Lobby of the House of Commons. Emmeline, who had been thrown to the floor by over-zealous policemen, was not arrested. All the others, save Charlotte Despard, were tried and sentenced as common criminals to two months' imprisonment. When Sylvia went to the court to protest against this treatment, she was thrown out into the street and arrested, tried and sentenced to two weeks' imprisonment. Each one of her daughters had now been imprisoned for the cause their mother had initiated.

On February 13th 1907 the WSPU set up a Women's Parliament in Caxton Hall, opposite the House of Commons, as an alternative to the latter and in direct opposition to it both physically and politically. Caxton Hall was to become the no-woman's land between constitutionals and militancy as speakers used the meetings held there to drum up support for militant activities. Those present at the first Women's Parliament, timed as usual to coincide with the opening of a new session in Parliament, listened carefully to reports from the House of Commons. When it transpired that, yet again, votes for women had been omitted from the parliamentary agenda, members of the WSPU marched across the road to deliver their suffrage resolution, only to be rebuffed by mounted police. After a battle lasting several hours, approximately fifty women, including Christabel and Sylvia, were arrested, and given two weeks' imprisonment. From this time on the hall would be used not merely as a meeting place, but as a militant base for suffragettes trying to deliver petitions to the House of Commons.

However, Emmeline Pankhurst's reputation as a violent militant can cause historians to overlook those occasions when she was all for compromise and advocated peaceful protest. For, throughout the WSPU militant campaign, she organised peaceful and legal as well as violent and illegal activities. Indeed, it could be argued that she contributed as much to the suffrage campaign by her non-militant work as by her advocacy of militancy. She was a busy, and effective, speaker, arguing her case with eloquence and remarkable cool and targeting her speeches to each audience. All who listened to her spoke of her soft, deep and mesmeric voice, still with a slight Lancashire lilt, that could be heard in the biggest meeting halls and even outside. Outdoor meetings were held every Sunday during the summer in London's Hyde Park and attracted more than 5,000 people each week. Other large meetings took place in Preston, Bury, Bristol, Portsmouth, Southampton, Leicester, Nottingham, Edinburgh, Bristol, Bradford and Hull. These meetings were successful even when it was decided in 1907 to charge people entrance fees in order to cover costs and raise funds for the WSPU.[25] Meetings were well co-ordinated. Emmeline Pankhurst was obviously the main attraction, but working-class women and representatives from professional occupations often shared the platform. Suffragettes were urged to inform 'Kensington how the Working Women in the North live ... to make the rich and idle women realise the difficulties of poor women'.[26] WSPU members were encouraged to do all they could for the suffrage cause: to offer hospitality to provincial delegates when they visited London; to join Tea Table Committees; to arrange Drawing-Room Meetings, Evening Parties, At Homes and Garden Parties; to become speakers; to recruit their friends; to buy and disseminate literature; to attend meetings; and if all that was a bit too much, simply to wear the Votes for Women badge.[27]

TACTICAL VOTING: ELECTION POLICY AND PRACTICE

Emmeline Pankhurst and the WSPU were not the first, and were by no means the last, to advocate tactical voting. With the Liberal Party firmly in power, she and the WSPU continued and consolidated the same disruptive tactics at by-elections as they had adopted for the 1906 general election. Electoral militancy was not indiscriminate. Initially it was targeted against the Liberals. Indeed, the WSPU opposed Liberal candidates regardless of their commitment to women's suffrage. This at first seems odd, especially when 420 Liberal MPs pledged their support. However, it must be remembered that for most of this period Emmeline was a staunch supporter of the ILP and the newly formed Labour Party and regarded the Liberals not just as the party in office which denied the vote to women, but as her chief political enemy.

The policy of the WSPU, largely initiated by Christabel, was therefore to oppose Liberal candidates at any by-election because the Liberal government refused to enfranchise women. Even government nominees who were in favour of women's franchise were opposed, because they belonged to the Liberal Party whose rank and file members voted as the party leaders bid them to.[28] At every by-election where a Liberal candidate was in the field, members of the WSPU were present to urge the electorate to vote against him. This policy was justified even when the individual MP was in favour of women's suffrage, because each represented, was nominated by and pledged to support the Liberals. Once elected, each MP sat on the government benches and voted with the government on issues which arose. The WSPU policy was based upon the practice of the Liberal leaders rather than the promises of private members. Emmeline even opposed those who voted for private members' bills in support of votes for women, thus displaying a remarkable political perspicuity. She all too quickly realised that private members' bills brought forward by sympathetic MPs were unlikely to be successful, as no bill ever became law unless the government supported it. The WSPU, and Emmeline Pankhurst, believed that individual MPs were powerless and that votes for women could only be gained by obtaining the support of the government itself. Moreover, she was very clearly aware that similar disruptive tactics by the Irish Party had defeated her late husband. In this respect, as in many others, her earlier experiences informed her later political actions, and she merely copied the successful tactics of another political agitator. Although Richard Pankhurst had been a great supporter of Irish Home Rule, he was, as a Liberal candidate, opposed by the Irish Party and defeated along with many MPs in the great Liberal defeat of the late nineteenth century.

Not surprisingly, this policy was criticised because it was seen to favour Conservative right-wing candidates rather than the left. Emmeline insisted that the defeat of the Liberal candidate would not deprive the government of power since it had a great majority in the House of Commons. Instead, it would indicate to the government that it must abide by Liberal principles. The WSPU, she argued, was not fighting against the government because it was Liberal but because it refused to enact Liberal principles by giving women the vote. Consequently, Conservative candidates often won by-elections, partly because of dissatisfaction with the Liberal government and partly because of suffragette opposition.

At Cockermouth, Cumberland, which was the first by-election at which this policy was put into effect, the Pankhursts refused to canvas for the ILP candidate, preferring to campaign for women's suffrage and to fight against the Liberals. Nevertheless, the WSPU did not always ignore Labour candidates. If MPs put women's suffrage before party politics, they gained suffragette support. In July 1907 Emmeline Pankhurst canvassed for an independent socialist candidate in the Colne Valley because he was a keen suffragist and critical of the close relationship between the Labour and Liberal parties.

From this time on, the WSPU was to focus on contesting Liberals at every possible by-election. At the Hull by-election in November 1907 Emmeline worked hard to defeat the government candidate, Mr Guy Wilson, who ran against Sir G. Trout Bartley (Conservative) and James Holmes (Labour). Despite the exceptionally poor weather – cold winds and sea fogs – she spoke at midday meetings at factory gates, at the docks, in Corporation Fields as well as at special meetings for women only. An indefatigable speaker, she would extemporise rather than read from a written text. On Saturday November 23rd 1907, a few days before polling day, she addressed brass-founders as they left their work for the weekend, imploring them not to vote for the Liberal candidate. Unfortunately, such actions must have created some confusion in the minds of voters since the Liberal candidate, Mr Wilson, was invited to speak at women's suffrage meetings held under the auspices of the NUWSS. In a letter to a local newspaper she defended her policy, arguing that the only way to get votes for women was to oppose a candidate who, 'while professing to be in favour of women's Suffrage, is seeking election in order to support a Government which taxes women and legislates for them, and obstinately refuses to give them representation'.[29]

Emmeline Pankhurst and the WSPU continually challenged the Liberals at by-elections, arguing that the Liberals had betrayed Liberal principles by denying women the right of citizenship. The NUWSS was criticised for supporting Liberal candidates and adopting 'a policy which cut right across that of the WSPU'.[30] In turn, the NUWSS argued that the WSPU's blanket opposition to Liberal candidates was politically inappropriate. Leading NUWSS figures wrote to the *Daily News* in January 1906 condemning the actions of 'these few violent women who have injured the reputation of women politicians in Lancashire. The disturbances were not planned by working women, but by a small clique.' Of course, the upshot of these differences in political strategy led to a situation in which the WSPU opposed the same candidate that the NUWSS was canvassing for, leading to great confusion in the minds of some voters. The WSPU, rather than the NUWSS, proved to be more successful for, as *Vanity Fair* stated, 'the ladies are carrying by-election after by-election for the Conservatives.'[31]

RESIGNATIONS

In 1907 the actions of Emmeline Pankhurst and the WSPU led to three forced resignations. Firstly, her own suffragette activity had made her position as Registrar untenable, even with the help of her sister Mary who acted as her deputy, and she was forced to resign her paid work. She had been warned by the Registrar General that her suffragette activities were incompatible with her official post, so rather than give up politics she gave up her job. This was another occasion when her political commitments and beliefs overrode any worries about personal financial security. Indeed, she expressed herself all too willing to give up pensionable employment for a political campaign that was just beginning, and that, as with her other suffrage involvements, might conceivably founder. So, with all her daughters employed and her son apprenticed to a builder, Emmeline Pankhurst left home. She packed up her personal belongings, got rid of her books, papers and other items that might clutter up her life, and moved to London to live at the Inns of Court hotel. From then on, almost until she left England after the war, she was to live an itinerant existence with no personal property other than her clothes, no furniture and no permanent base. To sacrifice so much at the age of 49, the women's suffrage cause must have been very captivating. She could not afford to fail.

Secondly, Emmeline was forced to resign from the ILP. Although her political beliefs remained identical with its programme, she had pointedly refused to endorse the Labour Party candidate at a by-election held in Cockermouth. These events split the Manchester ILP into two: the Central Branch (Manchester) which refused to condemn her actions and a new City Branch (Manchester) which put a resolution forward at the ILP Conference to censure her. At this time, her popularity among party members was still vast and she drew much support. 'I was quite overcome by the response on the part of the men at the Conference to my declaration of independence ... I was deeply touched.'[32] Eventually, however, the tensions between following a party line and forging ahead with new WSPU policy became too great. On September 14th 1907 she wrote to the ILP, using all the familiar socialist terms of address:

> Dear Comrade, I write to resign my membership of the Independent Labour Party. I take this step not because my convictions have changed. I am still a Socialist and in sympathy with the objects of the Party, but I am convinced that until women are men's political equals my first duty is to work independently of party for the political freedom of my sex. With heartiest wishes for the party's welfare, I remain fraternally yours, Emmeline Pankhurst.[33]

When she left the ILP, she was castigated for abandoning her socialist principles – indeed, she still comes in for criticism about this from contemporary historians. However, her resignation was a political strategy not an ideological shift, and she remained supportive of the Labour Party long after she had officially resigned. The Labour Party, formed from the Labour Representation Committee (itself an association of affiliated bodies such as the ILP and trade unions), was initially seen to be sympathetic to women's suffrage. Gradually, as Emmeline realised that the Labour Party was only lukewarm in its commitment, her support for the Party waned and she directed the same kind of attack against Labour as against the Liberals. Again, she was (and continues to be) criticised for this assault on the Labour Party. However, it was the party as much as Emmeline that had changed. She maintained that the Labour Party was virtually indistinguishable from the Liberal Party, as it became increasingly associated with Liberal Party policies. In 1903 the Labour leader Ramsay MacDonald made a 'secret' electoral pact with the Liberals, which divided up constituencies and committed the Labour Party to supporting any future Liberal government. In return, the Liberals promised not to oppose the Labour Party candidate in thirty constituencies. By 1908 the attitude of the Labour MPs on education, on imperialism, on free trade, on trade union reform and, most importantly to Emmeline, on women's suffrage was virtually indistinguishable from that of the Liberal Party in office. She had left the Liberal Party to join the ILP because of its radical promise, so the relationship between the Liberal Party and the Labour Party was seen to be an 'unholy alliance'. Emmeline Pankhurst therefore only broke with the Labour Party when it was seen to have abandoned its original aims.

Emmeline may have deserted the Labour Party but she never abandoned her allegiance to working-class women.[34] Of course, in its early years the WSPU recruited greater numbers of working-class than middle-class women – the roots of the movement lay in the Labour politics of the north of England rather than the Conservative salons of the south. The WSPU was set up specifically for working-class women and between 1903 and 1906 did valuable propaganda work in the textile towns. When the WSPU moved to London in 1906, working-class women were thought to have receded into the background to be replaced by women of an entirely different social class. Indeed, the WSPU is said to have concentrated on attracting middle and upper-class women into the organisation to the exclusion of working-class women. Admittedly, there is a great deal of truth in this assumption. Richer, more influential women joined in quite large numbers and the general image of the WSPU was that of a middle and upper-class movement. As Emmeline told an American audience, 'one of the things which gives strength to our agitation is that the women who are taking an active part in it are not the poorest women, are not the overworked women; they are the women who are held to be fortunate. Those women have taken up this fight for their own sake but also for the sake of the women less fortunate than themselves.'[35] In a political movement which relied upon the unpaid work of women, only those who were economically independent or married to men who were financially secure could afford to engage in many forms of political action.

We must remember, however, that the class composition of the WSPU was more heterogeneous than popular opinion suggests. Not all leading suffragettes were from patrician stock – there were a number who had impeccable working-class origins. The most famous of all was Annie Kenney, a cotton worker recruited at a WSPU meeting in Oldham, who became Christabel Pankhurst's confidante. The leading Scottish suffragette Jessie Stephens came from a working-class background and when interviewed later in life insisted there were 'a tremendous number of working-class women' involved in the WSPU.[36] Emma Sproson, a postman's wife from Wolverhampton, was imprisoned in 1907 for trying to force an entrance to the House of Commons in order to deliver a suffrage petition. To encourage working-class membership the WSPU did not have a definite subscription and members were encouraged to give what they could afford. As Emmeline Pankhurst noted, the WSPU had 'many members who really can't afford to pay anything at all.'[37]

Even when the WSPU's headquarters moved to London, there is evidence that it continued to target working-class women. Both Annie Kenney and Sylvia Pankhurst were sent to London to organise the campaign in the capital and spent most of their time in working-class districts; the first London branch of the WSPU was formed at Canning Town in the East End. The membership of this branch, known later as the East London Federation of Suffragettes (ELFS), was entirely working class, and it continued to be a part of the WSPU (albeit a problem one) until its official split in February 1914. Moreover, even in London the WSPU's strength lay with its local branches as much as with its headquarters, being active in the working-class areas of Woolwich, Lewisham and Greenwich. In the provinces, too, the WSPU tried to recruit working-class women. At one dinner-hour meeting outside a factory in the Black Country one woman was heard to remark: 'Aye, Martha did ye ever hear the like of it; isn't it grand! To think of those ladies working for the likes of us.'[38] Moreover, working-class women were amongst the paid workers of the WSPU, thus making it possible for them to remain active in the campaign.

The third resignation involved Emmeline's old friends and colleagues Charlotte Despard and Teresa Billington-Greig. In the heady atmosphere of Edwardian Britain, Emmeline believed that she could afford neither the trappings nor the substance of democracy. As militancy escalated, she tightened the reins of her leadership, refusing to discuss or accommodate differences among the suffragettes. With a strong belief in her own historic purpose, Emmeline brooked no opposition. According to Ethel Smyth, if you offended her 'on a vital point, you would have to be very dead indeed before she would really forgive you.' She had no time to 'cultivate mental habits and emotional reactions usual in ordinary intercourse'. When chastised for not being affectionate to others or caring as much as they did, she remarked: 'I don't suppose any one who cares tremendously about a cause has much to give to individuals.' She once remarked that 'if there are heads to be cut off in the office it's always I who have to do it'.[39] Loyalty to people was not high on the list of Emmeline Pankhurst's priorities, for her loyalty was to her principles.

Adhering to ideals rather than individuals, she rejected even those close to her if they disagreed.

In one sense, there was nothing new in her behaviour since the suffrage movement had been riven with personal rivalries and political schisms since its inception. Throughout her life Emmeline had either left organisations she was critical of or, in the case of her own organisation, encouraged others to leave. She had already given up her job and her home to develop the WSPU into an organisation capable of opposing the government, so when she encountered opposition from within she acted swiftly. In 1907 the first of a number of shattering splits in the WSPU took place, provoked by personal conflict, ideological differences and disagreements over political practice. These occurred not because the suffragette leader had an autocratic or even vindictive disposition – she did not – but because of her organisational theory. Unlike Millicent Fawcett, the leader of the NUWSS, who with tact, diplomacy and patience managed to weld a group of women together effectively and develop a consensus, Emmeline Pankhurst was a charismatic leader. In her view, the WSPU was to be a fighting organisation not a discussion group with a multitude of committees, motions to be carried and amendments to be heard, all of which would slow down the action. She wanted to be able to respond very quickly to events and to be free to make up policy in the midst of turmoil and potential confusion, which a leader of a bureaucratic organisation like the NUWSS would be unable to do.

In 1907 she failed to quell a potentially lethal revolt among WSPU leaders, two of whom challenged what they perceived to be the allegedly ever-growing autocracy of the Pankhurst family and their acolytes by demanding that an already agreed constitutional reform be enacted. There was no attempt by Emmeline to adopt a conciliatory tone; she no longer felt the need for a constitution and felt little instinctive loyalty to colleagues who disagreed with her. Moreover, the two rebel leaders, Charlotte Despard and Teresa Billington-Greig, wanted to continue to support Labour Party candidates in elections, whereas by this time the WSPU was strictly non-party. By the end of 1907 Emmeline Pankhurst was fully committed to political independence, urging her followers that 'if you are tied to any men's political party you must break that tie before you come into this movement .... For in this movement women are pledged to independence of all political parties till the vote is won.'[40]. More importantly, she had never been, was not and would never be one to compromise; in the past she had rejected her father and resigned from various organisations over matters of principle, and there was no way she would leave the one she had herself founded. She wrote to her daughter Sylvia: 'as for the TBG affair we have just to face her and put her in her place.'[41] The rest of the Committee and the membership agreed, and so in September 1907 Charlotte Despard, Teresa Billington and several others broke away from the WSPU to form the Women's Freedom League (WFL). In a letter to Elizabeth Robins, Emmeline said she 'thought it best' for them to form their own society, stating that the *Morning Post* gave the most accurate account of what happened. 'As soon as Mrs Despard's letter reached the papers,' she wrote, 'reporters swarmed into our office for information. We said as little as possible and they have made as much of what we said as they could.'[42] Two days later, on September 15th 1907, she wrote again to Elizabeth Robins: 'We wired you yesterday because we thought the time had come to issue the official statement (the only one) in reply to the seceders. Every member of the Committee approved and we wished to have your approval also …. We do not intend to discuss the matter any further either in the press or elsewhere but think having made this one official statement we should entirely disregard what other people do or say and go on with the Union work.'

CONCLUSION

The split within the WSPU prompted the first of many charges against Emmeline Pankhurst for despotic and peremptory behaviour: loyalty to the leader was expected, with WSPU members accountable to her alone. Her dictatorial behaviour was highly offensive to women fighting for democratic reforms. As justification for her allegedly domineering status, she could point to a measure of achievement for she was undoubtedly responsible for transforming and certainly revitalising what had been a moribund suffrage movement. In so doing, the WSPU became the best-known, although not necessarily the best-loved, suffrage organisation. Moreover, in her defence she insisted that local WSPUs had complete autonomy subject to their acceptance of the policies of the National WSPU.[43]

Emmeline Pankhurst may have been willing to lose certain friends, but she was very protective of others. Elizabeth Robins sent an early draft of her novel *The Convert* for her comments. The heroine, who has a child out of wedlock and is gradually converted to women's suffrage, is given the name Christian. Emmeline Pankhurst wrote: 'I hope you will forgive me if I put two points of view as to the heroine .... First the personal one. The heroine has a past she is no worse for that perhaps she is better for it, such experience trains a fine nature but her name suggests Christabel's. Now Christabel has no past still many people might connect the imaginary with the real and say that Christian's story is Christabel's .... Second I don't think she should be an actual member of the WSPU but a sympathiser .... Don't think me squeamish but our work is so difficult as it is without paragraphs in the papers suggesting that this person or that is the heroine.'[44] Elizabeth Robins took the hint and the heroine's name was changed to Vida. Emmeline may have expelled rebellious elements from her organisations but she was capable of a generous sensitivity to the feelings of loyal supporters. In the same letter she asked Elizabeth Robins to make one further change: 'The only thing that fails is Mrs Martel. She is such a good soul really and I fear she will recognise the portrait. I would not have her hurt for worlds. She is horribly sensitive under that surface that repels you. Is it too late either to cut her out or alter her beyond recognition? She is such a good fighter and came to our side when we had so few friends. In spite of her little ways which sometimes make me squirm I am very fond of her and I don't like to think of her being wounded.'[45]

Despite all the splits, the arrests, trials and imprisonments of her members, the year ended on an optimistic note, thus justifying her resignation as Registrar and her move to London. By the end of 1907 the WSPU occupied 21 rooms at the new headquarters at Clement's Inn and between 1906 and 1907 raised £3,000. It had held upwards of 5,000 meetings, fought thirteen by-elections and opened over 70 branches. The first issue of *Votes for Women*, financed and edited by the Pethick-Lawrences, had also appeared in October 1907 and set out in clear detail the aims of the movement. The first issue proclaimed: 'If you have any class feeling you must leave that behind. If you are tied to any men's political party you must break that tie .... The founders and leaders of the movement lead, the non-commissioned officers must carry out their instructions .... There is no compulsion to come into our ranks, but those who come must come as soldiers ready to march onwards in battle array.'[46] A portrait of Mrs Pankhurst was sent out to every new reader.[47]

Emmeline Pankhurst founded one of the most vibrant and dramatic female organisations ever known. Its aim was to gain the vote on the same terms as men, yet for her the vote was never merely an empty and showy proclamation of women's citizenship but a tool with which to improve the lives of all women, regardless of their class background. Throughout her leadership of the WSPU she remained steadfastly loyal to working-class women and their concerns. In this she mirrored many female philanthropists who believed that privileged women had a duty to help bring about social justice for those who were less fortunate than themselves. However, for Emmeline Pankhurst the vote, not charity, was the key to female emancipation and equality. She had already sacrificed a job, a pension and a home. In future years, she would also sacrifice her freedom and her health.

5

DEEDS AND WORDS 1908–09

The year 1908 was a watershed for Emmeline Pankhurst's militant strategies. In April Asquith, an uncompromising adversary and opponent of women's suffrage, replaced Campbell-Bannerman as Prime Minister. Soon after Asquith's appointment she prophesied an increase in militancy if the government remained obdurate to women's pleas for social justice, urging that it was imperative 'to stop the struggle before the women's movement got so big and powerful that they would not be able to control their forces'.[1] The spirit in woman today, Emmeline argued, could not be quenched for 'it is stronger than all earthly potentates and powers; it is stronger than all tyranny, cruelty, and oppression; it is stronger even than death itself.'[2] The religious fervour with which she declared this was self-evident and her words were prophetic. In the same year the first outbreak of window smashing occurred when Edith New and Mary Leigh broke the windows of 10 Downing Street.

It is sometimes assumed that the iconoclastic Emmeline Pankhurst, who marshalled her obedient membership to commit crimes, orchestrated this kind of behaviour. However, the first violent tactic of the suffragettes, breaking windows, was an impromptu act born of desperation rather than a coherent political strategy devised by the WSPU leaders. The suffragette leader, along with a group of elderly supporters, had just been evicted from the House of Commons, arrested, put on trial and sentenced to six weeks' imprisonment. Exasperated, Edith New and Mary Leigh smashed their windows in protest. Militancy such as this often began at a local level with a few ardent activists and was only adopted as WSPU policy when it received extensive support from the membership. For much of her time as leader of the WSPU, Emmeline wielded less power than her position, her followers or some historians suggest. Increasingly, the reins of policy-making were taken over by her daughter Christabel or else by the members themselves. One teacher who had been window breaking stated that 'Mrs Pankhurst is not responsible for my deed. While I love and honour her as a woman, she might have talked for an eternity and not moved me to militancy. It is the truths she tells.'[3]

Of course, the definition of militancy is a problematic one.[4] Militancy is an elastic concept which changed its meaning over the fifty or more years in which women campaigned for the vote; suffragists were considered militant in 1860 when they dared to speak at meetings yet by 1914 public speaking was seen to be quite acceptable female behaviour. Even so, peaceful protests would be considered extremely militant by certain sections of the population. In her novel *The Convert* Elizabeth Robins tells of how compromised her heroine, Vida, would be if she was found to listen to, let alone participate in, an outdoor political meeting. Concerned that acquaintances might recognise her listening to the suffragettes, Vida dresses up in her oldest clothes and wears a veiled hat to disguise herself. Emmeline, of course, brought up to fight for social injustice, had already engaged in most of the early WSPU activities while a political activist in Manchester. Her definition of militancy took on a different and unique form, transforming both the meaning of the word and its relationship to female action. Certainly, by 1914 WSPU militancy had reached new heights but it was a much slower process than is sometimes realised. Systematically militancy escalated: from heckling, to window breaking, to eventually arson. Moreover, the WSPU were not the only militant organisation since the WFL endorsed a policy of non-violent militancy by refusing to pay taxes and spoiling ballot papers in by-elections.[5] It was the use of violence, rather than militancy, that separated the WSPU from other suffrage groups.

Emmeline Pankhurst justified the escalation of this type of militancy by arguing that women, denied the vote, were being refused constitutional rights to gain it. She held her convictions strongly. That passion and conviction became even more evident in the suffragette years which followed. It was no use, she insisted, saying that women must hold meetings, send petitions and lobby members of Parliament since they had done this for fifty years. Peaceful protest, she maintained, was by now 'absolutely useless'. Before men got the vote, 'they asked for it nicely, and when they found that asking for it nicely did not give it to them they began to do things – they burned down public buildings, assaulted bishops and archbishops, and created a revolution.'[6] Repeatedly she held the Liberal government responsible for militancy, arguing that it was a rational response to the failure of the government to meet suffragette deputations, to the exclusion and eviction of women from Liberal meetings and to the intransigence of Asquith. The Liberal government, she claimed, was immune to conventional political strategy. Judges, under the direction of the government, had incited women to violence by denying them the right to petition. Had women been allowed to enter Parliament, Emmeline argued, there would have been no organised violence such as stone throwing. In a familiar refrain, she maintained that for the last thirty years she had tried constitutional methods but it had been of no use: she had presented petitions, held great public meetings, faced hostile mobs on street corners. She had taken militant action, because 'the condition of our sex is so deplorable that it is our duty even to break the law in order to call attention to the reasons why we do so'.[7]

Emmeline Pankhurst may have created history but she was also part of it. At the time of escalating WSPU militancy, Britain was experiencing one of the most turbulent periods in its history. A wave of industrial unrest was deluging the country, the House of Lords was in rebellion and there was mutiny in Ireland. Suffragette violence merely added another dimension to the growing dissatisfaction with the Liberal government and another element to the opposition forces with which it had to deal.

ARRESTS, TRIALS AND IMPRISONMENTS

Between 1908 and 1914 prison, and the threat of it, dominated Emmeline Pankhurst's life. Not surprisingly, given her advocacy and practice of militancy, she was constantly summonsed, arrested, tried and imprisoned, receiving six custodial sentences, undertaking twelve hunger strikes and going to prison fourteen times. If she insisted on forcing the government to grant women's suffrage, then the government was equally committed to not giving in to that force. At first she was convicted for crimes she herself had committed, but in the end, as leader of the WSPU, she was held responsible for the crimes of other suffragettes. The last six months of WSPU activity before the First World War were marked by her arrest, imprisonment, hunger and, sometimes, thirst strikes, subsequent release and rearrest.

Convictions

February 1908: 6 weeks for obstruction

October 1908: 3 months for inciting the public to rush the House of Commons; released before sentence expired

June 1909: Arrested for assaulting police officer; fined £5 or prison sentence. Fine paid by anonymous donor

Nov 1910 Black Friday: arrested in Downing Street but no charge made

March 1912: 2 months for attempted window breaking

May 1912: 9 months for conspiracy; released after five weeks

April 1913: Three years' penal servitude

Using Caxton Hall, the site of the first Women's Parliament, as a base, the first of these recurring scenarios took place on February 11th 1908, when she led a deputation to the Prime Minister in protest against the recent arrest, trial and conviction of fifty suffragettes. A few days earlier a number of suffragettes, hidden in two furniture vans, tried to gain entry to the House of Commons, only to be repelled by the police. Emmeline Pankhurst, recently arrived from opposing the Liberals in a by-election in South Leeds, challenged their resulting conviction and tried to deliver a protest resolution to the Prime Minister. The police refused to allow her and the other suffragettes entry to Parliament and charged them with obstruction. For this offence she was sentenced to six weeks' imprisonment on refusal to be bound over – as she left the court she shouted out 'Votes for Women'.

Eight months later she was arrested charged and imprisoned once more. The events that led to her second imprisonment took place on October 12th 1908 when, along with Christabel and Flora Drummond, she was served with a summons for conduct likely to provoke a breach of the peace. They had distributed a leaflet encouraging others to 'rush' the House of Commons (i.e. to make a special effort to enter the House of Commons, by force if necessary, in order to speak to the Prime Minister, whether he wished to hear them or not). To drum up support for this event Emmeline Pankhurst had spoken at a public meeting in Trafalgar Square on Sunday October 11th. A kite emblazoned with *Votes for Women* flew from a launch – ritualistically decked out with flags and bunting in purple, white and green – moored outside the House of Commons as a visible gibe to MPs that the suffragettes were about to invade. When charged with causing a breach of the peace, Emmeline Pankhurst and the rest of the accused refused to obey the summons and instead led a protest meeting at the Queen's Hall. When the meeting had finished, they were issued with a further summons to attend Bow Street Court the following morning. This again they refused to do and a warrant was issued for their arrest.

Emmeline Pankhurst, Christabel and Flora Drummond were eventually arrested late at night when the courts had already risen, could not be given bail and were detained in the police cells. Lady Constance Lytton was allowed to visit the prisoners and met the suffragette heroine for the first time. Faced with a night in the cells with only wooden benches for beds, Emmeline was anxious for a good night's sleep in order to prepare for her defence the next day. Constance Lytton left to try to get them released. Although she was unsuccessful, she returned with food and blankets only to find the prisoners sitting at a table laid with silver and candlesticks with three waiters serving them. The feast, along with comfortable beds, had been sent in from the Savoy Hotel at the request of a sympathetic MP.

At the trial, which eventually took place on October 14th 1908, Emmeline Pankhurst pleaded that she was fighting for the vote for wider social and legal justice for women. It was here that she spoke more of her famous words: 'We are here not because we are law-breakers; we are here in our efforts to become law-makers.'[8] It was to be one of the first big political trials of the WSPU with all the usual attendant paraphernalia. Two leading Liberal MPs, Lloyd George and Herbert Gladstone, were called as witnesses. Liberalism, as much as militancy, was on trial. Lloyd George, no doubt mindful of his reputation as a reforming radical, was careful not to give evidence that might lead to the conviction of the suffragettes. After listening to the MPs and twenty-two other witnesses, the magistrate refused to hear any further evidence and bound Emmeline and Flora Drummond over to keep the peace for twelve months or face three months' imprisonment in the Second Division. Christabel was given ten weeks. It was to be Christabel's last prison experience, though not her mother's.

Prison was largely for the poor, not for the law-breaking middle-class intelligentsia. Prisoners, drawn from the ranks of the more desperate section of the working class, were generally incarcerated for petty theft, habitual drunkenness, prostitution, non-payment of fines, infanticide and occasionally murder. White collar crime and commercial crime, or at least their prosecution, were rare. Few middle-class women were found in prison so by deliberately courting arrest and trial the suffragettes broke every conceivable code of gender – and class – conduct.

Once sentenced, Emmeline could have been allocated to one of three prison categories: the First Division, the Second Division or the Third Division. First Division prisoners were granted the status of political prisoners because they had been convicted of a political rather than a criminal offence. Second Division prisoners were deemed to be reputable characters from respectable family backgrounds, and Third Division prisoners were defined as the criminal element of society long-past redemption. Each class of prisoner received different treatment dependent on the category. First Division prisoners were permitted to wear their own clothes, provide their own food and receive as many visitors, books and letters as they wished. Second and Third Division prisoners were less fortunate; they were provided with prison food and had their correspondence, reading material and visitors severely circumscribed. In March 1906 the then Home Secretary, Herbert Gladstone, granted suffragette prisoners the right to be placed in the First Division, and by 1907 suffragettes claimed that first-class treatment was the established rule. In 1908 Herbert Gladstone revoked his previous decision and refused to authorise political offender status for suffragette prisoners, declaring that he had no power to interfere with the discretion of the magistrates who were responsible for sentencing procedures.[9] Each case, he argued, must be examined separately because prison status was dependent on each individual's character and the nature of the offence committed. The upshot of the new ruling was that suffragettes committing the same crime could be placed in different divisions depending on the magistrate's appraisal of their character and class background, the political influence of their families or the media publicity that surrounded them.

Emmeline was sentenced to the Second Division on both occasions she was imprisoned. At this time conditions were atrocious for second and third class prisoners. On entry to prison she would have been undressed, searched and forced to relinquish all her personal belongings, then taken a bath and put on a prison uniform. Second Division prisoners wore green serge dresses; those in the third class wore brown. All prisoners were forced to wear white caps, blue and white check aprons and were given one big blue and white check handkerchief a week. Underwear was coarse, ill-fitting and usually stained, and prisoners were given thick, shapeless black stockings with red stripes to wear without garters or suspenders. Each prisoner wore a large badge made of yellow cloth bearing the number of the cell and the letter and number of the prison block. Emmeline Pankhurst's was H24. When she had dressed, she was given sheets for her bed, a toothbrush and a Bible, then taken to a cell that contained a wooden bed, a straw mattress and pillow, two narrow blankets and a woollen quilt. In the corner of the cell was a shelf upon which, in regimental order, was a pint pot for the prisoner's food, a wooden spoon, a wooden salt cellar, a piece of soap and a case containing the prison rules. Opposite the cell door a basin, a slop pail which was used as a lavatory, a small container of water, a plate and a dustpan, a bath brick, cleaning rags and two sweeping brushes were to be found. At 6 a.m. each morning she would have to empty her 'slop' bucket. Later she would be given a bucket of water and a scrubbing brush with which to scrub all the tins, the bed, the stool and shelves and the cell floor. Breakfast, generally consisting of a pint of oatmeal gruel and 6oz brown bread, was brought round to each cell. At about 8.30 a.m. the prisoners went to chapel: First Division prisoners sat behind a screen at the side of the altar; Second Division prisoners sat near the front of the chapel and the rest of the chapel was occupied by the Third Division. After chapel prisoners were expected to work; second class prisoners were given sewing or knitting to do – Emmeline spent her time knitting socks – whereas those in the Third Division were given the most menial tasks such as cleaning the corridors and other parts of the prison. Second Division prisoners were allowed to exercise every day by marching slowly and silently in single file around a paved yard. Lunch, served between 11 a.m. and 12 noon would consist of potatoes, beans and some meat for Second Division prisoners.[10] Those in the Third Division received oatmeal porridge and bread. Supper, consisting of more gruel and bread, was at 5 p.m.

For someone as fastidious as Emmeline prison must have been especially hideous, with its dirty baths and gross inhumanities. She spoke of the egregious conditions of 'civilised torture of solitary confinement and absolute silence' and how she had felt 'like a human being in the process of being turned into a wild beast'. Although some wardresses spoke kindly, most of them adopted a special prison voice, ' a voice of iron',[11] which only changed when the prisoners were about to be released. Not surprisingly, the suffragette leader was not an ideal prisoner and refused to conform to what she believed to be an unjust system. Never a compliant or obedient person, it was unlikely that she would be a docile prisoner and indeed continually provoked the prison authorities. In her second imprisonment she refused to abide by Second Division regulations and broke the rule of silence by speaking openly to her daughter Christabel. She was punished for this, given solitary confinement and made to exercise alone. Eventually, because of the intervention of the Home Secretary, who in turn had been pressurised by awkward questions in the House of Commons, she was given permission to 'associate' with her daughter for an hour each day. She was released on December 22nd 1908 after having spent eight weeks in the prison infirmary. According to the radical journalist Henry Woodd Nevinson, her first prison experience had shaken her profoundly and 'she was more overcome and tearful',[12] but this did not deter her. After her first two imprisonments, although she was arrested, tried and convicted, she was not imprisoned again until 1912.

Her third arrest took place in June 1909 when she – once more – led a small deputation to take a petition to the King. Asquith – yet again – refused to see them. Henry Woodd Nevinson called this event 'The Battle of Westminster'. The deputation, he wrote, 'was small, not more than seven ... in front of them all, walked Mrs Pankhurst, pale but proud and perfectly calm, with that look of courage and persistency on her face ... the crowd received her with overwhelming enthusiasm. She walked fast. Mounted police cleared the way in front; police marched on each side of her, keeping back the excited admirers.'[13] On this occasion, she deliberately hit Police Inspector Jarvis twice so that she would be charged with assault. She was duly arrested and taken to Bow Street on

June 30th 1909 with over 100 other suffragettes who had broken windows in protest at the failure of the deputation. When her case was eventually heard, she was given a fine of £5 or one month in the Second Division, but when an anonymous donor paid her fine, she was released to continue with her suffrage work. Other suffragettes were less fortunate; in 1909 294 women were arrested, 163 imprisoned, 110 went on hunger strike and 36 were force-fed.[14]

Once imprisoned, suffragettes continually campaigned for First Division status, claiming that whereas common criminals broke the law for personal reasons, WSPU activists broke the law to bring about democratic reform so must therefore be classed as political prisoners.[15] According to Ethel Smyth, WSPU members were urged to exaggerate their ailments, to complain against prison conditions such as dirty bath water, and to 'generally render the lives of the Governor and his visiting magistrates intolerable'.[16] Prison conditions did improve in 1909. Suffragettes were placed in new cells, given nightdresses, a new toothbrush, new shoes, a brush and comb, underclothing which, though patched and worn, was no longer smelling foul or evil, their own earthenware mug and plate and metal spoon in place of a common tin used by all.[17] Even so, Emmeline wrote to *The Times* in August 1909 complaining that prison cells were damp, verminous and smelling of sewage. 'One of the ex-prisoners', she complained, was put in a cell containing 'offensive sanitary accommodation' (a euphemism for buckets full of urine and excreta) and 'is at present undergoing medical treatment for the vermin which got into her hair'.[18]

CAMPAIGNING ON THE HUSTINGS

The WSPU continued with their by-election policies. In January 1908 the first by-election to be fought that year took place in Newton Abbot, Mid-Devon. Here the Liberal candidate suffered if not a crushing defeat, then certainly a significant one, reducing his once healthy majority to a loss. Emmeline Pankhurst claimed that the Conservatives beat the Liberals because 'life-long Radicals decided to vote against that government which by its treatment of the women's claim to enfranchisement is violating the chief principle of Liberalism'.[19] The local Liberal Party definitely attributed its Mid-Devon defeat to the adverse action of militant suffragists.[20] Consequently, an infuriated mob of Newton Abbott Liberals wreaked vengeance upon the WSPU, attacking Emmeline and Mrs Martell by pouncing on them and handling them roughly. When the two women tried to escape this hostile crowd, they were savagely assaulted and 'both fell to the ground, when they were struck on the head several times and also kicked .... Mrs Martell had marks on her throat where she was "collared" and was badly bruised, as was also Mrs Pankhurst who had her ankle injured.'[21] When they ultimately got away, both 'presented rather a pitiful appearance, being plastered with mud and with their dresses in a very bedraggled state'.

Despite suffering from heavy injuries, Emmeline spoke at two meetings at the Drill Hall in Ross, Herefordshire, a few days later. Again, the Liberal candidate was defeated. As soon as the by-election in Hereford was over, she left to help in the Worcester campaign. As we can see from the following timetable of meetings, the WSPU were still speaking largely at working-class, rather than middle-class, venues.

'Votes for Women' February 1908 Campaign in Worcester

Jan. 30th	GWR Fitting Depot 1 p.m.
	Williamson Tinsmiths' Works 1 p.m.
	Diglis Pickling Works 7.30 p.m.
Jan. 31st	GWR Shed Depot 1 p.m.
	Evans' Vinegar Works 1 p.m.
	Co-operative Hall Women's Meeting (Mrs Pankhurst) 3 p.m.
	Sheep Market (Mrs Pankhurst) 7.30 p.m.
Feb. 3rd	Dent's Glove Works 1.30 p.m.
	Webb's Horsehare Works 1.30 p.m.
	Baylis's Printing Works 7.30 p.m.
	Sheep Market 7.30 p.m.
Feb. 4th	Heens and Froude's Iron Works 1.30 p.m.
	Lea and Perrin's Sauce Factory 1.30 p.m.
	Sheep Market 7.30 p.m.
Feb. 5th	Bourne and Grove's Saw Mills 1.30 p.m.
	McNaught's Carriage Works 1.30 p.m.
	Star Hotel Reception 3 p.m. (Mrs Pankhurst)

At the by-election in Leeds in March 1908, just after her first imprisonment, Emmeline again played a principal role, leading an evening
torch-lit procession to Hunslet Moor. She spoke of the meeting where
'thousands and thousands of men and women followed our procession
through the streets, and attended our meeting ... and among them all
there was hardly a sneer or a jeer, not even from among the Liberals
themselves'.[22] Here the Liberals retained their seat – but with a much-
reduced majority. The most crushing blow to the Liberals came on April
25th 1908, when the Conservative candidate in a North-west
Manchester by-election defeated Winston Churchill when he was
appointed as a cabinet minister. Constitutional practice at the time
decreed that newly appointed ministers had to stand for re-election. In
his acceptance speech the Conservative candidate acknowledged the
'assistance I have received from those ladies who are sometimes laughed
at, but who, I think, will now be feared by Mr Churchill, the
Suffragists. They have worked well for the cause they have at heart, and
I congratulate them on having taken some part of the victory.'[23]
Churchill next stood for the safer seat of Dundee, won despite opposition from the suffragettes, and was returned to Parliament.

Less than two months later Emmeline organised another by-election
campaign in Montrose, Scotland. She visited the suffrage centres of
Burghs, Montrose, Arbroath, Brechin and Forfar, speaking at meetings
and encouraging members. On one occasion fishermen at Arbroath covered their lorry with a new sail and a strip of new green carpet.
'Standing in this was a table draped with a red cover and on it two
bowls of primroses and a vase of daffodils, a very large glass of water and
a tumbler! There were three cushioned chairs and waving on this a flag
and a banner.'[24] At Montrose she experienced very different treatment
when the Provost (the main official in the town), who was also the
Liberal candidate's election agent, directed the police to remove suffragettes violently from the polling booths. A few days later she was in
Stirling and Dunfermline speaking in halls and open-air meetings at
various points of the city and holding dinner hour meetings daily. The
crowds at the indoor meetings sometimes reached 2,000. In June 1908
she was again on the by-election trail, this time in Pudsey in Yorkshire,
where the Liberal Party candidate, as in so many other by-elections contested by the WSPU, was defeated. Emmeline believed that the success
of the WSPU in Pudsey was because the constituency lay close to Leeds

and Bradford, where the movement was strong and well organised.[25] One month later she planned the campaign to defeat the Liberal candidate at Haverfordwest in Pembrokeshire, Wales. In her view, this particular by-election was a critical one because it was a Welsh constituency very sympathetic to David Lloyd George.[26] At a meeting in nearby St David's Emmeline Pankhurst attracted an audience of approximately 2,000, not all of whom were sympathetic.[27] When she held at a meeting at St Dogmells the crowd came armed with stones, sods and curses to hurl at her and she only narrowly missed being injured. The Liberals retained their seat.

In 1909 the WSPU contested nine by-elections: Croydon, East Edinburgh, Sheffield, Stratford-on-Avon, Cleveland, Derbyshire, Dumfries, Bermondsey and St George's in the East. In three of these elections the Liberals lost their seat and in three others the previous Liberal majority was significantly reduced.[28] Emmeline Pankhurst toured the country, speaking at Torquay, Bristol and Plymouth in February 1909 before moving on to Scotland.

As usual, the WSPU members were encouraged to disrupt Liberal meetings and 'in spite of buffetings, chuckings-out, scoldings, and even imprisonment, raise their shrill battle-cry of "Votes for Women" wherever a Minister is found addressing his fellow countrymen. Banged, barred and bolted doors do not keep them out of ticket meetings. They pervade the by-elections with their supplications to the electors to vote against the Government.'[29] Such was their success that the generally sympathetic editor of the *Guardian*, C.P. Scott, was prompted to write to Emmeline, pleading for her not to interrupt a forthcoming meeting arranged by the Manchester Liberal Federation in support of women's suffrage: 'We can't even ask a Cabinet Minister to come unless we can assure him that no sort of interruption will be sanctioned by the WSPU and that instructions to this effect will be issued from headquarters.'[30] She ignored his pleas and militancy continued.

When speaking, the suffragette leader always buttressed her arguments with anecdotes about the suffrage campaigns or referred to local or international themes. Emmeline always tried to establish some affinity with her audiences by discussing issues relevant to them. In a meeting held on February 12th 1909 in the rather sedate and Conservative seaside town of Torquay, she was given an enthusiastic reception by the large female audience. The meeting, held at Bath Hall, was decorated with the colours of the WSPU and she was presented with a basket and bouquet of purple and white flowers with asparagus sprays. In her speech, and very aware of the audience's employment, she drew attention to the inequity between men and women landlords. 'In a town like Torquay,' she said, 'there must be hundreds of women earning their livelihoods by letting apartments' who paid rates and taxes on their properties yet were all denied the vote.[31]

Sometimes she used a magic lantern to illustrate her talk. Slides illustrating the activities of the WSPU – processions to the House of Commons, women being arrested, Mrs Drummond addressing MPs from a launch on the Thames – were used. One slide had the words 'The man who stands between women and the vote' next to a portrait of Mr Asquith.[32] As befitting a party leader, and her celebrity status, she drew large audiences, for example in Aberdeen where visitors came from the 'hotel and the surrounding houses, the village shopkeepers left their shops, eager-faced ghillies brought their dogs down and even the children listened with great attention'.[33]

PEACEFUL PROTEST

Despite her unconventional behaviour, Emmeline Pankhurst always dressed well, although the public image of suffragettes and their portrayal in some of the press was often unsympathetic. The typical description of a hypothetical suffragette was a 'gaunt, unprepossessing female of uncertain age, with a raucous voice, and a truculent demeanour, who invariably seems to wear elastic-sided boots, and to carry a big "gampy" umbrella, which she uses as occasion demands either to brandish ferociously by way of emphasising her arguments, or to belabour any unfortunate member of the opposite sex who happens to displease her'.[34] The leaders of the WSPU undermined this stereotype by their strict attention to dress. As Cecily Hamilton, suffragette playwright, stated: 'In the WSPU the coat-and-skirt effect was not favoured; all suggestion of the masculine was carefully avoided, and the outfit of a militant setting forth to smash windows would probably include picture hat.'[35] Emmeline certainly spent a lot of time on her physical appearance: 'she always looked charming and had such a sweet smile and was so thoroughly feminine'.[36] *Votes for Women* urged suffragettes to follow their leader's example: 'The suffragette of today is dainty and precise in her dress; indeed, she has a feeling that, for the honour of the cause she represents, she must live up to her highest ideals in all respects. Dress with her is therefore of the utmost importance.'[37] Indeed, Emmeline's distinctive, restrained and elegant style of dress was constantly remarked upon.

Emmeline Pankhurst, and the other suffragettes, seemed to be a paradox: beautifully dressed and coiffured while at the same time rejecting other feminine values. It is this paradox which appeals: the suffragettes' physical *appearance* was the very essence of femininity whereas their violent physical *actions* challenged and undermined Edwardian notions of that same quality of being female. On the one hand, suffragettes conformed to the romantic ideal of womanhood by paying a great deal of attention to appearance and wearing white flimsy dresses with violet corsages. On the other hand, they challenged the very essence of womanhood by their militant behaviour. Femininity with violence was an exciting combination. However, wearing stylish clothes was no mere fashion statement; it was a uniform – indeed one might say battle-dress – which signified membership of the WSPU. Once a woman wore the colours purple, white and green, she was immediately identified as a suffragette. On important lecture tours Emmeline Pankhurst always wore the same heliotrope dress in the same way as a general might wear his battle-dress on state occasions. She was always 'attractively gowned in a mauve Empire frock of velvet. The lining of the large, loose sleeves was of a dull shade of green, little green dangels hanging from them, green embroidery in the front with a hint of a green skirt of the same shade beneath, and with the white of the close-fitting undersleeves and the neck'.[38] The WSPU also distributed their own medals for bravery for suffragettes to wear on their uniform on public occasions. After her first two prison sentences in 1908, Emmeline was presented with a necklace of amethysts, pearls and emeralds as a token of WSPU esteem. She was also presented with a silver badge of honour on which her prison cell number, H24, was engraved: H for hospital, 2 for the floor, and 4 for the cell number. All these she wore proudly on the suffragette equivalent of state occasions. This seeming paradox, however, can be understood by realising that Emmeline wanted to feminise politics, not to masculinise women who wished to be engaged in political activity. Equally, she was defensive about the accusation that suffragettes were unnatural and mannish.

Best known for her advocacy of militancy, Emmeline Pankhurst and the WSPU continued to press on with conventional methods of protest, from speaking in public, to organising demonstrations, exhibitions and other activities. From 1907, under the editorship of the Pethick-Lawrences, *Votes for Women* reported suffrage events. Moreover, as events became increasingly dramatic so circulation increased. By April 1908 circulation had reached 5,000 a month and *Votes for Women* was issued weekly rather than monthly and the price reduced from 3d to 1d as a result of its ever-increasing distribution record. In 1909 the Pethick-Lawrences handed over the paper to the WSPU and it was enlarged from sixteen to twenty-four pages. By the end of the year circulation had increased to 20,000 and the pages increased to thirty-two in order to meet the numerous demands for space.

Demonstrations were occasions to show off suffragette style as well as promote the cause.[39] On Sunday June 21st 1908 Emmeline Pankhurst led the first of the WSPU's large-scale demonstrations, during which seven different processions congregated in Hyde Park to be entertained by over eighty female speakers. Seventy-four special, and more importantly cheap, trains brought delegates to London. Working-class women travelled from all parts of the country to join the demonstrations. Train fares cost between 2s 9d and 11s, a weekly wage for working women, so working-class women were subsidised.[40] A high tea at 9d a head was served before the return journey. Given her theatricality, she must have enjoyed the new-style demonstration co-ordinated by Emmeline Pethick-Lawrence, in which the colours purple, white and green made an eye-catching display. In a rather derogatory manner, Emmeline Pankhurst noted that the WSPU demonstration had more working-class women than the demonstration organised by the NUWSS the week before. As one of the main speakers, she attracted a crowd of about 5,000. When all the speeches had finished, bugles were blown as a signal for everyone to shout out 'Votes for Women' and so a great roar was heard from the multitude of women assembled. The press congratulated the WSPU on its immaculate organisation. As *The Referee* commented: 'Suffragette Sunday promises to give us a white whirl of womanhood … the petticoat has beaten the bifurcated garment …. The fine flower of British womanhood was there to demand the enfranchisement of the sex. It came, it was seen, and it conquered.'[41] Over half a million people had come to the Hyde Park meeting place. Of course, not all were sympathetic and both Emmeline and Christabel were heckled.

Following the success of the June event in London, various demonstrations were held in the provinces. On Saturday July 18th 1908 a great demonstration of between 20,000 and 30,000 people took place in Nottingham. At the mass meetings that inevitably followed these demonstrations Emmeline was often subjected to continuous interruption by the disruptive element in the crowd. 'It was in vain that she tried to make her voice heard above the din going on. When there was a temporary lull she pleaded for a fair hearing, but the only answer she received was the chorus of some popular song and jeering and shouting continued throughout the time she was on her feet. Only now and again was she able to speak a completed sentence.'[42] A demonstration that same month in Manchester that drew 50,000 people proved to be much more successful, largely because of her past local reputation. She strongly urged that 'if women had sufficient intelligence to earn their own living, to pay their rent, and obey the laws which 7½ million men in the country were making for them, surely in justice the vote should be given to them. Concerning the laws affecting women and children, marriage and divorce, women had a special right to make their voices heard .... The conditions of women's labour, she contended, also called for the making audible of women's views. Then there was the protection of their sex. There should be something more than a law that only protected the virtue of the working-class girl up to the age of 16, whereas among the wealthier classes the mere property of a person was protected up to the age of 21. They claimed also that the interests of children demanded that women should have the vote.'[43] Later that month she led a demonstration of approximately a hundred thousand people from Victoria Square, Leeds, to Woodhouse Moor, where she initially encountered hostility and ridicule. She also supported the Sweated Industries Exhibition, which publicised the plight of low-paid women workers.

As well as participating in demonstrations, she spoke at meetings all around the country, most often to working-class women. Some meetings were held on Sundays because it was the only day that working women could attend. Members were urged to recruit tea-shop girls and to make 'a point of visiting every teashop in their district .... The same applies to all shops.'[44] Shop assistants, mill workers, nurses, ex-pupil teachers, working-class wives, postal telegraphists, tailoresses and leading Trade Unionists would be invited to speak at these events.[45] Emmeline's speeches generally focused on the concerns of working-class women. At a meeting in Edinburgh she drew attention to the necessity of the vote for working women, arguing that the Sweating Bill introduced that year by Churchill was a by-product of suffragette agitation.[46] By now she was an exceptionally accomplished speaker, at ease with any audience, capable of tackling hecklers and of targeting her speech to any given audience. She was a strong draw at the Free Public Meetings. These were held every Monday afternoon between 3 and 5 p.m. at the London Pavilion in Piccadilly Circus and on Thursday evenings between 8 and 10 p.m. at the Steinway Hall or Essex Hall. Meetings were also held regularly at the Albert Hall. Ticket prices ranged from 6d to 2s 6d but there was free admission on the night to women. Gradually, of course, meetings became opportunities for militant action. It is doubtful if any other suffragette, save her daughter Christabel, rivalled her in oratorical effectiveness. Henry Nevinson thought Emmeline's speech at the Albert Hall in March 1908 was excellent, although he considered that Christabel was the 'greatest living speaker.'[47] In speech after speech she kept before women the issues at stake in the suffrage and communicated to them her confidence in eventual victory.

Each year Emmeline led a 'Self-denial' week, an idea copied from the Salvation Army, in which WSPU members were urged to make a special effort to raise funds for the movement by personal sacrifices. During this week WSPU members and sympathisers made and sold sweets and flower arrangements, swept crossings, bootblacked and collected money from City offices, singers and violinists amused theatre queues and artists drew pictures on public pavements in an attempt to raise money.[48] One man went without his cigars for a week, one woman gave up butter, and one went without her servant, while another took a barrel organ around Torquay.[49]

During the summer months, when Parliament was in recess, suffrage activity tended to decrease so that everyone could rest until Parliament reconvened in the autumn.[50] During this period the WSPU targeted holiday towns like Felixstowe, Cowes, Ilfracombe, Torquay, Dartmoor and resorts in the Isle of Man and Scotland. In August 1909 they visited 33 different resort towns to sell their literature and gain support for votes for women.

In 1909 an exhibition held at the Prince's Skating Rink, London, drew thousands of visitors. Here Emmeline sat selling millinery among stalls selling flowers, sweets and children's toys; bands and entertainment were provided by the Actresses' Franchise League; there were jujitsu demonstrations and reconstructions of polling booths and prison cells. Cartoon models of Asquith in the dock and Emmeline Pethick-Lawrence in the witness box were added attractions, as were demonstrations by Cradley Heath chain-makers.[51] Exhibitions may have provided the suffragettes with a short respite from militancy but the suffragette leader was obviously bored, probably missing the excitement of militancy, possibly not wanting to be reminded of the failure of other business ventures. As Rachel Ferguson, founder of the young WSPU, stated: 'I can hear her uninterested, dispassionate voice saying "Pretty little vase, a shilling".'[52]

CONCLUSION

Under Emmeline's leadership the WSPU flourished, thus justifying her commitment to this new-style organisation. In 1908 through to 1909 its income tripled, the number of paid organisers doubled to thirty, the office at Clement's Inn grew larger and eleven regional offices were set up in Aberdeen, Birmingham, Bristol, Edinburgh, Glasgow, Leeds, Manchester, Newcastle, Preston, Rochdale and even Torquay. The Monday afternoon meetings attracted audiences of up to a thousand, and the circulation of *Votes for Women* increased considerably. Militancy had escalated. A Young Hot Bloods group, known as the YHB, was formed for suffragettes under the age of 30 who were committed to 'danger duty'. Emmeline Pankhurst witnessed suffragettes such as these engage in ever-increasing militancy. They heckled cabinet ministers at meetings, led deputations to Parliament, chained themselves to the railings outside 10 Downing Street or to the grilles of the Ladies' Gallery in the House of Commons, embarked on window smashing, rubber-stamped graffiti on parliamentary walls and threw stones from rooftops.

In response, suffragettes were banned from Liberal meetings, and those engaged in illegal activities were duly imprisoned. Instead of succumbing to prison treatment some went on hunger strike, initially being released when their condition was critical. The first hunger striker, Miss Wallace Dunlop, had been arrested in July 1909 for writing extracts from the Bill of Rights on to the walls of the House of Commons and sentenced to one month's imprisonment in the Second Division. Considering herself to be a political prisoner, Wallace Dunlop refused to be treated as a common criminal and went on hunger strike to secure full rights as political prisoners for herself and others. Succeeding prisoners followed her example, including Lady Constance Lytton and the family of Emmeline Pankhurst. When her sister Mary was imprisoned, Emmeline wrote to C.P. Scott, editor of the *Manchester Guardian*, pleading with him to use his influence with the Home Secretary to help her sister, who 'is very weak and depressed and I fear that although in hospital she will have better food and more comfortable surroundings these will do her little good because she is in absolute solitude ... know from my own experience how nerve destroying the solitary system is'.[53] Mary Clarke was not alone. Sylvia Pankhurst, though never Christabel, went on several hunger and thirst strikes. From this time on, large numbers of suffragettes refused to eat, both as a protest against the prison regulations,[54] and because they were subjected to being treated as common criminals rather than political prisoners. In theory, the hunger strike was not 'the official policy of the Union but a matter for individual decision'.[55] In practice, this was not the case. Marie Brackenbury remembers being told by Emmeline 'not to hunger strike on this occasion'.[56]

At first, hunger strikers were released from prison, but soon the government introduced force-feeding for women who consistently refused to eat. In September 1909 the first woman was force-fed at Winsom Green Prison, Birmingham. Almost immediately Emmeline and Christabel Pankhurst, accompanied by their solicitor, left for Birmingham to act on behalf of the prisoners, only to be informed that they would not be allowed to do so. Forcible feeding, despite some public protest, was to be used repeatedly on large numbers of hunger-striking suffragettes.

Other suffrage leaders disagreed with this new direction in suffrage activities. Ethel Snowden wrote to Millicent Fawcett that she was having a 'wordy duel' with Emmeline over the stone-throwing of the suffragettes but feared she was having little effect.[57] Millicent Fawcett replied that the NUWSS needed to distance itself from the WSPU and show that it stood for peaceful persuasion. The recent outbreak of criminal violence by the WSPU, she went on to say, 'was not caused by a few excitable members getting out of hand but was obviously premeditated